NAVIGATING

IMMIGRATION LAW

A Handbook for HR Professionals

Raju Mahajan, Esq.

Immigration & Employment Attorney

Norah Global Media

To request permissions, contact the publisher at https://www.norahmedia.com

ISBN: 978-1-962957-11-3 (Ebook)
ISBN: 978-1-962957-12-0 (Paperback)
ISBN: 978-1-962957-13-7 (Hardcover)
ISBN: 978-1-962957-14-4 (Audiobook)

Library of Congress Control Number: 2024927401

Norah Global Media, LLC
4520 East West Highway, Suite 750
Bethesda, MD 20814

The number of immigrants in the American workplace increases every year. I dedicate this book to HR professionals everywhere who are on the frontlines of today's rapidly shifting global landscape. Your work is vital to the success of organizations. It is my hope that this book helps make your work easier and gives you the confidence to navigate the challenges ahead.

Table of Contents

Preface

As I began writing this book, one thought kept coming back to me: Managing people is, without a doubt, one of the toughest jobs out there. It's more than just supervising tasks or managing processes—it's about understanding individuals, motivating them, and somehow aligning everyone toward a common goal. In today's globalized world, where people from all corners of the globe come together with vastly different cultures, backgrounds, and perspectives, this challenge has only intensified.

HR professionals are at the forefront of this challenge. They're the ones responsible for ensuring that large organizations run smoothly, even when they're managing incredibly diverse teams. And with the rise of global migration, their role has grown even more complex. In the US especially, where people from countless countries converge in the workforce, HR professionals are required not only to manage this diversity but also to navigate the labyrinth of employment and immigration laws. It's a daunting task, especially when the regulations are constantly evolving.

This book was born from a desire to help lighten that load. I've organized key immigration laws in a way that is straightforward and accessible, aiming to give HR professionals the tools they need to manage this aspect of their work with greater ease. While this book is not intended to replace legal counsel, I hope it provides a solid foundation to help navigate the complexities of immigration in the workplace.

Of course, immigration laws are ever-changing. Procedures, fees, and policies can shift overnight, so I always strongly recommend checking the latest information from reliable sources like the US Citizenship and Immigration Services, available at http://www.uscis.gov. This book is designed to give clarity to the options available and their corresponding processes, but it's essential to verify the most up-to-date details when making decisions.

I'm also eager to hear your thoughts. If you find areas that need refinement or updating as laws change, please don't hesitate to reach out. I'm committed to keeping this book as relevant and useful as possible.

Finally, I want to express my appreciation to HR professionals everywhere. Your work is vital to the success of organizations, especially in today's rapidly shifting global landscape. It's my hope that this book helps make your work a little bit easier and gives you the confidence to navigate the challenges ahead.

Thank you for picking up this book. I hope it serves you well.

Raju Mahajan, Esq.

Part One:

Common Visas Relating to Employment

Chapter One:

Employment-Related Matters
for the F1-Visa

⎯⎯⎯⎯⎯⎯ ▱ ⎯⎯⎯⎯⎯⎯

A ccording to Statista[1], there were over one million international students in the US during the 2022-2023 school year—with approximately 77% of these scholars specializing in the areas of science, technology, engineering, and math (STEM). While most of these students plan to return to their home countries after completing their degrees, increasing market demands and employment shortages, especially in STEM careers, have provided opportunities for many students to remain in the US and seek employment-based visas after graduation.

There are also several options for foreign scholars to work in the US *while* on their student visas, both prior to and after the completion of their degree programs. Often these employment experiences help students connect with US employers who wish to later sponsor them for employment-based visas or even US permanent residence.

---

[1] https://www.statista.com

This chapter focuses on the particulars of obtaining and maintaining F-1 student status, the different employment and practical training opportunities available to international students, and the rules and regulations (for both students and employers) that govern each student work program.

1. Work Authorization for F-1 Students

Overview

International students have several opportunities to work in the US while in F-1 status. They can work on campus (On-Campus Employment), do an internship related to their major (CPT), or gain practical experience either while enrolled in a degree program (Pre-Completion OPT) or after finishing their degree (Post-Completion OPT). Each option has distinct rules and time limits that students need to follow carefully to maintain their visa status.

On-Campus Employment

Students on an F-1 visa can work on campus for up to twenty (20) hours per week during the semester and full-time during school breaks. This type of work does not require special permission, as it is part of an F-1 student's visa privileges. However, students should keep track of their work details, such as the type of work, employer name, school affiliation, and hours per week, because they might need this information for a future employment-based visa application. Their school official (DSO) might also keep records of their on-campus work, but it is not mandatory.

2. Curricular Practical Training (CPT)

Overview

Students on an F-1 visa can engage in work related to their major under Curricular Practical Training (CPT). CPT is considered part of their study plan, so students must do any CPT before finishing all their courses and before their I-20 expires.

To be approved for CPT, international students need to obtain permission from a school official, typically the DSO. The DSO will provide a letter stating the name of the employer, the type of work, and the start and end dates of the CPT. Students can have more than one CPT at the same time, but they must get permission for each one. It is advisable that students apply for CPT at least two (2) weeks before they want to start working.

It is important to note that if students work full-time CPT for one (1) year or more, they will become ineligible for any Optional Practical Training (OPT) later. On the other hand, students who use less than twelve (12) months of full-time CPT will remain eligible for their full twelve (12) months of OPT.

Day 1 CPT

Day 1 CPT refers to a specific regulation found in select master's or doctoral programs that permits international students to initiate CPT immediately upon starting their studies. Essentially, this means they can participate in internships or employment right from the beginning of their academic program, often on the first day. Educational

3

institutions offering programs with this feature are commonly referred to as *Day 1 CPT Universities.*

It is crucial to recognize that Day 1 CPT is not uniformly available across all educational institutions and programs. Prospective students should thoroughly research their chosen universities and program policies before applying. Eligibility for Day 1 CPT varies depending on specific institutional and programmatic factors.

Eligibility Criteria for Day 1 CPT

- Student status: The student must hold international graduate status in the US and be enrolled in a master's or doctoral degree program.
- Full-time enrollment: The student must maintain full-time enrollment throughout their academic program.
- Alignment with curriculum: The employment responsibilities must directly correlate with the student's academic program.
- CPT approval: Commencing internships or employment is only permitted after the school has granted approval for CPT, and it should align with the specified CPT start date on the I-20 form.

Requirements for CPT Application

- Satisfactory academic progress: Students must maintain a cumulative GPA of 3.0 or higher.
- Employment offer: Students must secure a job offer before applying for CPT authorization.

- Field of study: Employment opportunities through CPT are restricted to the students' central area of study.
- Timely application: Most educational institutions establish deadlines for CPT applications. It is crucial to adhere to these deadlines to ensure timely processing.

3. Optional Practical Training (OPT)

Overview

F-1 students can gain work experience related to their major subject through an Optional Practical Training (OPT) program.

There are four types of OPT:

1. Pre-completion OPT: Obtained before completing the degree.
2. Post-completion OPT: Obtained after completing the degree.
3. STEM OPT Extension: An additional twenty-four (24) months available for degrees in science, technology, engineering, or mathematics.
4. Cap-Gap OPT Extension: Extension until the start date of H-1B employment (if an H-1B petition is pending).

Note: International students can apply for OPT at each degree level, but they are limited to only two (2) STEM extensions.

To apply for OPT, students need to get a recommendation from their DSO and then submit Form I-765 to USCIS. While it is not required to have a job offer before applying for OPT, it is still recommended to secure one to avoid delays and potentially falling out of status.

Additionally, students must wait to receive an Employment Authorization Document (EAD) from USCIS before they can begin working. STEM OPT applicants, however, can continue working after their initial OPT ends if the application for extension was filed before the initial OPT expired and they have received the Receipt Notice from USCIS. The timing for applying for OPT depends on which type of OPT the student wants to pursue and when they plan to finish their degree.

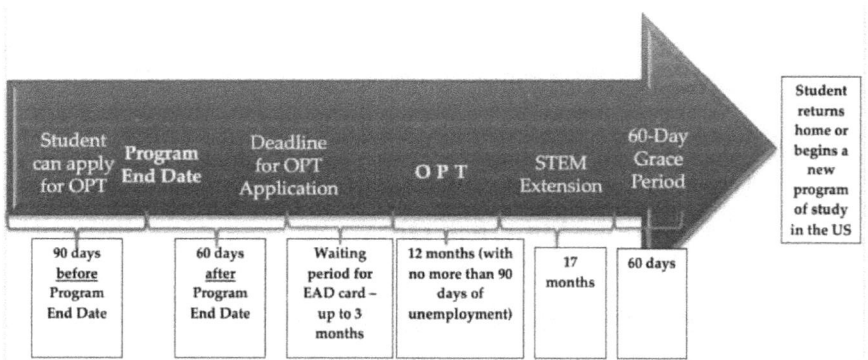

Student can apply for OPT	Program End Date	Deadline for OPT Application	OPT	STEM Extension	60-Day Grace Period	Student returns home or begins a new program of study in the US
90 days before Program End Date	60 days after Program End Date	Waiting period for EAD card – up to 3 months	12 months (with no more than 90 days of unemployment)	17 months	60 days	

General OPT Application Requirements for USCIS:

1. Completed Form I-765 with the required application fee (payable by check or money order or also by credit or debit card using Form G-1450).
2. Two (2) passport-style photos taken in the past thirty (30) days.

3. Completed Form G-1145.
4. Photocopy of I-20 with DSO's OPT recommendation issued within the last thirty (30) days for post-completion OPT and within the last sixty (60) days for STEM extension.
5. Photocopies of all previous I-20 forms.
6. Photocopy of most recent visa.
7. Photocopy of Form I-94 Arrival/Departure Record.
8. Photocopy of any previously issued Employment Authorization Documents (EADs).

Pre-Completion OPT

Before finishing their degrees, international students can apply for pre-completion OPT (Optional Practical Training used before graduation) if they want to work in the US. This type of work authorization is related to their major subject. Students are eligible to apply for pre-completion OPT after having studied full-time for at least one (1) year at a SEVIS-approved university. They don't need to have been in F-1 status for the whole year, as long as they were in another valid nonimmigrant status.

With pre-completion OPT, students may work part-time (twenty (20) hours or less) during the semester and full-time during school breaks. However, students should know that utilizing pre-completion OPT will reduce the time they have left for post-completion OPT.

When a student chooses to utilize pre-completion OPT, the amount of time they spend working is subtracted from their overall 12-month OPT allowance (not including STEM or Cap-Gap extensions). This subtraction is done proportionally. For example, if a student works full-time under pre-completion OPT, each month of work deducts a full month from their 12-month total—a 1:1 ratio. However, if a student works part-time under pre-completion OPT (twenty (20) hours per week or less), each month of work only deducts half a month from their 12-month total, resulting in a 1:2 ratio. Thus, part-time work during pre-completion OPT consumes the available OPT time at a slower rate than full-time work. Nevertheless, it might be better to use CPT instead of pre-completion OPT if a student wants to start working prior to graduation. Also, CPT does not require USCIS approval, which can be a lengthy and costly process.

Post-Completion OPT

After international students complete their degrees, they can apply for post-completion OPT if they want to work in the US in a job related to their major. They can apply for post-completion OPT even if they don't have a job offer yet, but they must report any changes in their name, address, or employment status while on OPT. They can get twelve (12) months of post-completion OPT if they have not used any pre-completion OPT time. Students can work full-time or part-time with post-completion OPT but must work at least twenty (20) hours per week.

24-Month (STEM) OPT Extension

If an international student has a STEM degree, they can apply for a 24-month extension of their OPT. Their I-20 form must show that the degree is in one of the STEM fields approved by the US Department of Homeland Security (DHS). A full list of the approved fields of study can be found on the

DHS website. Sometimes, an older STEM degree may be used to apply for the extension; however, the students have to meet the following conditions:

1. Their most recent degree is from an accredited school and is also SEVIS-certified,
2. Their older STEM degree is not more than ten (10) years old when they apply, and
3. Their older STEM degree is also on the DHS list of approved fields of study when they apply.

Students should apply for the STEM extension as soon as possible within ninety (90) days before their post-completion OPT ends. This way, they can obtain their new work permit card (EAD) with the STEM extension dates before their post-completion OPT expires and avoid any gaps in their employment. However, if a student applies for the STEM extension in a timely manner but doesn't receive their new card before the post-completion OPT ends, they can still continue to work for up to one hundred and eighty (180) days or until USCIS makes a decision on their application, assuming they maintain a valid I-9 form with their employer. After completing their STEM extension period, students then have sixty (60) days to leave the US or change their status.

If students want to extend their OPT for an additional twenty-four (24) months, they need to make sure their employer can provide at least twenty (20) hours of work per week as well as offer training with specific goals in mind. Students must also fill out a Form I-983 with their employer and send it to their DSO. It is also possible for students to be self-employed if they meet all the necessary regulations, such as being part of the E-Verify system (a program that checks if someone is allowed to work in the US, see Chapter 7).

Cap-Gap OPT Extension

Sometimes an employer may want to sponsor a student for H-1B status, a nonimmigrant visa category for skilled workers (see Chapter 2 for more details). If students are on OPT or a STEM extension, they may need a Cap-Gap OPT extension to keep working until their H-1B status becomes active. This extension covers the gap between the OPT and H-1B. Eligibility for this extension is contingent upon the student having applied for a change of status to H-1B before their OPT expires.

4. Severe Economic Hardship Employment

Overview

Certain F-1 students can request a "Severe Economic Hardship EAD" with their DSO's recommendation (Form I-20 with recommendation for Economic Hardship EAD). However, the student must have been enrolled for at least a full academic year before applying for this benefit. The student will also have to prove that they have severe economic hardship. SEVP defines "severe economic hardship" as something that was caused by unforeseen circumstances beyond the student's control that make it difficult for them to continue their studies without additional income.

These circumstances may include:

- Loss of financial aid or on-campus employment through no fault of their own.
- Substantial changes in the exchange rate or value of the currency upon which they depend.
- Increases in tuition or living costs.
- Unexpected changes in the financial state of their source of funds.
- Medical bills.
- Other substantial and unexpected expenses.

The applicant must also prove why on-campus employment is unavailable or insufficient to meet their financial needs. This EAD is valid for a maximum of one (1) year or until the end date of their study program, whichever is shorter. It may also be valid until their circumstances improve, but not to exceed one (1) year. The student can maintain their F-1 status while they work. They can also renew the EAD after one (1) year if their situation has not changed. As long as the student remains at the same school, the one-year validity period will be in effect. If they change schools at any point, their EAD will no longer be valid.

5. Reinstatement of F-1 Status

Overview

When an international student fails to maintain their F-1 status and their SEVIS Immigration Record is terminated, they will be considered out-of-status and no longer eligible for any benefits under F-1 status.

In this case, the student can apply to USCIS to regain their F-1 status through a process called Application for F-1 Status Reinstatement. Following the reinstatement approval, the student will resume active F-1 status and regain eligibility for all qualifying status benefits.

Eligibility Requirements for Reinstatement of F-1 Status

- The student must not have been out of status for more than five (5) months at the time of filing the application. If the student fails to file a reinstatement application within five (5) months, they must demonstrate that the failure to apply for reinstatement within this period was due to exceptional circumstances.
- The student is currently pursuing or intending to pursue a full course of study in the immediate future at the school that issued the I-20.
- The student must not have any record of willful or repeated violation of USCIS regulation.
- The student has not engaged in unauthorized employment.
- The student's F-1 status violation must have resulted from extraordinary circumstances beyond their control.
- The student is not deportable on any ground other than overstaying or failing to maintain status.

NOTE: Examples of circumstances that could be considered beyond the applicant's control might encompass the following situations:

- A severe illness or injury
- A natural disaster
- Inadvertence or oversight
- The closure of the educational institution
- Lack of assistance from the educational institution

Timeline

A student should apply for reinstatement as soon as possible after their SEVIS record is terminated. As mentioned above, an application for reinstatement cannot be made more than five (5) months after the SEVIS termination, except in the aforesaid exceptional circumstances.

Cost

If filing within five (5) months of the date of SEVIS termination, the applicant will need to pay a USCIS fee of $470 for the application.

If the applicant has been out of status for more than five (5) months, they will also have to pay the SEVIS fee again.

Forms to be Completed for the Reinstatement Application

- Form I-539 (Application to Extend/Change Nonimmigrant Status)
- Form G-1145 (E-Notification of Application/Petition Acceptance)

Reinstatement Application Procedure

1. First, the applicant needs to submit an online I-20 request to International Students Services (ISS).

2. Once the new I-20 is received, the applicant can prepare and submit the reinstatement application (Form I-539) together with the required documents to USCIS. (See below for list of required documents).
3. Once USCIS receives the application, it will be checked for completeness. USCIS may request the applicant to provide more information or evidence to support their application. USCIS may also ask the applicant to provide the original copies of certain documents.
4. The applicant may also be requested to appear at a USCIS office for an interview based on the application.
5. USCIS will determine and notify the applicant of their decision, indicating whether or not the applicant has established eligibility for the reinstatement.

Required Documents in Support of Application

1. USCIS filing fee of $470 (which includes the biometrics fee).
2. Letter of Explanation detailing why the applicant fell out of student status and the consequences the applicant will face if they are not reinstated.
3. Letter of Motivation explaining why the applicant is pursuing or intending to pursue a full course of study.
4. Copy of passport.
5. Copy of visa.
6. Copy of Form I-94.
7. Copy of new Form I-20 issued for reinstatement request.
8. Copy of all previously issued I-20s.
9. Evidence of financial support.
10. Graduate Assistantship Offer Letter (if applicable).

11. Savings and bank statements covering expenses of at least one (1) year for the applicant.
12. Bank statement from the sponsor (if applicable) covering expenses of at least one (1) year and/or tax return and/or W-2 and signed letter of sponsorship.

Additional/Optional Documents

- Copy of Admission Offer Letter.
- Class schedule.
- Proof of home residency outside the US.
- Relevant email correspondence.
- Any other documents that might help demonstrate that the reasons for the applicant's SEVIS termination were beyond their control and why their F-1 status needs to be reinstated.

NOTE: The more evidence one can show in support of the application, the better the chances of it being approved.

Application Processing Time

A reinstatement application may take up to five (5) months to process.

Requirements While Reinstatement is Pending

1. The applicant must maintain full-time enrollment for each semester.
2. The applicant should not travel outside of the US while the reinstatement application is pending. The application for reinstatement is considered abandoned if the applicant leaves the US while the reinstatement is still being processed.

Conclusion

The reader should now have a clearer understanding of how a foreign national may obtain and maintain valid F-1 student status as well as the different options for authorized employment while in this status. Nevertheless, it is highly recommended to consult with an attorney for a more extensive and thorough insight.

Chapter Two:

Employment-Based Nonimmigrant Visas

———————— ⊐ ————————

For companies interested in hiring a foreign worker or workers, unless the prospective employee is a lawful US permanent resident (green card holder) or possesses an EAD (work permit), the employer will most likely need to petition the USCIS for an employment-based visa on behalf of the individual.

Employment-based visas fall into two categories: nonimmigrant (NIV) and immigrant (IV). Employment-based NIVs are generally short-term (with some possibilities for extension), and the employee is limited to working only for the petitioning employer and in the petitioned position or capacity. However, nonimmigrant visas are generally easier, faster, less expensive, and more readily available to a wider range of workers than immigrant visas.

In the case of nonimmigrant visas (NIVs), these offer a way for employers to get a foreign employee on board quickly and see if they are a fit for the position or give the employee a chance to gain additional experience and/or skills needed to qualify for an immigrant visa. An NIV is also the better option for short-term employment arrangements or when the foreign worker does not have plans to reside permanently in the US.

In addition, most nonimmigrant visa categories allow the spouse and minor children of the employee to join them in the US as well. In some cases, the family members may be permitted to work or attend school in the US. There are also quite a number of NIV categories, so some individuals may find that they are eligible for more than one type of NIV. As such, it is important to understand the specifics of each visa category, including length of stay, availability, cost, processing time, and other benefits or limitations in order to select the best option.

This chapter will present the different categories of employment-based nonimmigrant visas, as this is the most common first (and perhaps only) step in hiring a foreign employee.

1. Specialty Occupation Visa: H-1B

What is an H-1B visa?

Introduced in 1990 with the intention of expanding the labor pool in the US, the H-1B is a nonimmigrant visa category that allows US employers to temporarily employ qualified foreign workers in specialty occupations. According to I.N.A. § 101(a)(15)(H), 8 USC. § 1101(a)(15)(H), these occupations require specialized knowledge and typically include fields such as science, technology, engineering, and mathematics (STEM). However, this visa category is also accessible to individuals in a variety of other specialized fields, including finance, IT, accounting, legal services, and more. H-1B status is typically granted for an initial period of three (3) years, with the possibility of extension for up to an additional three (3) years (or more, in some cases).

The H-1B visa category is divided into three (3) classifications:

- H-1B (Specialty Occupations)
- H-1B2 (Researcher or Development Project Worker for a group/project monitored by the US Department of Defense)
- H-1B3 (Fashion Model)

H-1B: Specialty Occupations

Here we will go into more detail with respect to the first H-1B classification (Specialty Occupations) as it is by far the most widely petitioned of the three.

In a broader sense, there are two (2) main types of H-1B visas:

1. Cap-Subject H-1B Visa: The US government imposes an annual cap, or limit, on the number of H-1B visas that can be issued each fiscal year. If the number of applicants exceeds the number of visas available for a particular year (which has generally been the case in recent years), the applicants are selected through an H-1B lottery registration. As of Fiscal Year 2024, this cap is set at 85,000 visas.

This cap is divided into two (2) categories:

a. Regular Cap: This includes 65,000 visas for foreign workers with a bachelor's degree or equivalent.

b. Master's Cap: An additional 20,000 visas are reserved for individuals with a master's degree or higher from a US institution of higher education.

2. Cap-Exempt H-1B Visa: Certain employers and positions are exempt from the H-1B cap. This means they can petition for H-1B visas outside of the regular cap limits and do not need to go through the lottery registration process. Some examples of cap-exempt employers and positions include institutions of higher education (e.g., colleges and universities), non-profit research organizations associated with institutions of higher education, and government research organizations.

Read more: https://www.uscis.gov/working-in-the-united-states/h-1b-specialty-occupations

Key Features

The H-1B visa offers numerous perks for both employers and employees. Employers gain the advantage of sourcing skilled professionals globally, including immediate relatives, enhancing the talent pool and competitiveness of their business. Foreign employees, on the other hand, can legally work in the US for up to six (6) years, with potential extensions, providing stability and career opportunities.

Accompanying spouses and minor children can also join the H-1B recipient in the US. H-1B holders and their family members enjoy flexibility in travel and continuous residence in the US. In certain cases, spouses of H-1B holders may also obtain employment authorization in the US. Furthermore, H-1B employees have the option to change employers by filing a new petition at any time—fostering career growth and mobility.

In the case of job termination by the US employer, the employer has the obligation to cover the costs of the employee's return trip to their home country, providing a safety net for foreign employees, regardless of the reason for termination.

Overall, the H-1B visa program facilitates talent acquisition, career advancement, and international collaboration— benefiting both employers and employees alike.

Eligibility Requirements for an H-1B Visa

Qualifications of the Employee: To qualify for H-1B status, the employee (beneficiary) must possess the following:

- Education or experience: The beneficiary must possess a bachelor's degree or the equivalent work experience that is needed to qualify for the offered job. USCIS generally requires three (3) years of specialized training or work experience for every year of college not attended.
- Specialty occupation: The beneficiary must be coming to the US to perform services in a specialty occupation (see detailed description below) that requires a college degree or its equivalent in work experience.
- Job offer: The beneficiary must have a job offer from a US employer for work in the United States, with a wage offer that is either: (1) at least equivalent to the prevailing wage in the same geographic area for the same type of job, or (2) the actual wage paid to

similar workers at the petitioning employer, whichever is higher.

Criteria of a Specialty Occupation: The job itself must meet at least one (1) of the following criteria to be considered a specialty occupation:

- Educational Requirement: The position must require at least a bachelor's degree or equivalent as a minimum entry-level qualification.
- Industry Standard: The degree requirement must be common in the industry for similar positions among parallel organizations, or the duties of the position must be sufficiently complex to require a person with a degree to perform them.
- Employer's Normal Practice: The employer must generally require a degree or its equivalent for the position.
- Specialized Duties: The specific job duties must be so specialized and complex that the knowledge required to perform them is typically associated with a bachelor's degree or higher.

Eligibility Requirements for Employer: To sponsor an employee for an H-1B visa, the employer must meet these specific requirements:

- Legal Existence: The employer must be a US-based entity that is legally authorized to hire workers.
- Job Offer: Employers have to offer jobs that involve complex and specific tasks that are crucial for their business.

- Labor Condition Application (LCA): Employers need to file a Labor Condition Application with the Department of Labor and get it approved. This is to ensure that the wages and working conditions meet certain standards.
- Ability to Pay: Employers must show they have sufficient funds to pay the employee according to the LCA's requirements.
- Work Hours: The beneficiary is typically required to work full-time, although part-time employment may be permitted under certain circumstances.
- Minimum Wage: The employer must pay the beneficiary the prevailing wage for the occupation in the specific geographic area.

Validity of H-1B Visa and Extensions

An H-1B specialty occupation worker can be admitted for a period of up to three (3) years. This time frame can be extended, but it generally cannot exceed a total of six (6) years, with certain exceptions permitted under sections 104(c) and 106(a) of the American Competitiveness in the Twenty-First Century Act (AC21) as outlined in 8 CFR 214.2(h)(13)(iii)(D) and (E).

The types of extension are specified in the following categories:

1. H-1B Extension After the Initial Authorized Period: This discretionary process applies to individuals who want to extend beyond the initial period of authorized stay. If approved, this extension grants H-1B status for up to three (3) additional years, enabling the

beneficiary to stay legally in the US in H-1B status for up to six (6) years. H-1B visa holders who spent time abroad may also extend their stay by recapturing the time spent outside the US.

2. H-1B Extension Beyond the Six-Year Limit (AC21 Extension): Under sections 104 and 106 of the American Competitiveness in the 21st Century Act (AC 21), certain individuals may be eligible to extend their H-1B status beyond the standard six-year limit if they meet certain criteria. This typically applies if either an Alien Labor Certification (Form ETA 750A-B or ETA 9089) or an immigrant worker petition (Form I-140) was filed on their behalf at least three hundred and sixty-five (365) days prior. Their eligibility depends on the "priority date," which is the date of their labor certification application or the filing of an I-140 petition with USCIS. H-1B extensions can be granted until the labor certification or I-140 is adjudicated, and, if approved, one-year extensions are possible until an adjustment of status or immigrant visa application outcome is determined.

3. To apply for an extension beyond the six-year limit, the applicant needs to file Form I-129 along with evidence of their eligibility for an exemption from the H-1B cap and proof of the pending labor certification or I-140 immigrant petition.

4. H-1B Extension for Foreign Nationals Chargeable to Oversubscribed Countries: According to the American Competitiveness in the 21st Century Act (AC21), specifically section 104(c), H-1B visa holders who are

beneficiaries of approved employment-based (EB) petitions but cannot apply for adjustment of status due to per-country visa limitations can extend their nonimmigrant status until their adjustment of status application is processed. In this case, the I-140 petition must be approved for eligibility. Extensions are allowed for up to three (3) years at a time, with the possibility of multiple extensions if necessary.

5. To apply for an extension in this category, the applicant needs to file Form I-129 along with evidence of their eligibility for an exemption from the H-1B cap and proof of the approved immigrant petition. Additionally, USCIS guidance stresses the importance of providing proof of visa priority date and demonstrating the applicability of per-country visa limitations or overall unavailability of visa numbers.

Read More: https://www.uscis.gov/policy-manual/volume-7-part-e-chapter-5

H-1B Filing Process at a Glance

The H-1B visa filing process involves multiple stages depending on the type of application. Here is a general outline:

- **Lottery Registration:** Employers who fall under the Cap-Subject H-1B category need to go through the H-1B lottery registration process. Employers submit petitions on behalf of their prospective employees during this window. Here's how the H-1B lottery typically works:

- **Application Period:** USCIS usually accepts H-1B visa petitions for a limited period—typically during the first week of April each year. Employers submit petitions on behalf of their prospective employees during this window.
- **Cap Limit:** The H-1B visa program has an annual cap on the number of visas issued, which is set by the US Congress. As of 2024, this cap was 85,000 visas per fiscal year, with 65,000 reserved for regular H-1B applicants and an additional 20,000 reserved for individuals with advanced degrees from US universities.
- **Lottery Selection:** If the number of petitions received exceeds the annual cap, a random lottery is conducted to select the petitions that will be processed further. This means that even if an employer submits a petition on behalf of a prospective employee, there's no guarantee it will be accepted.
- **Random Selection Process:** USCIS uses a computer-generated random selection process to choose the petitions that will move forward.
- **Petition Submission:** The petition process is mostly the same for all categories of H-1B:
- **Labor Condition Application (LCA):** The US employer submits an LCA to the US Department of Labor via the iCert Web portal (http://icert.doleta.gov). The employer must also post a notice of this filing at the workplace.
- **USCIS Petition:** Once the LCA is approved, the employer files a petition for the foreign worker

(beneficiary) using USCIS Form I-129. If the beneficiary is already in the United States in a lawful status that allows a change to H-1B status, the petition can request this status change.

- **USCIS Review:** USCIS evaluates the petition to confirm it is complete and that the beneficiary satisfies the eligibility criteria for an H-1B visa. Upon approval, if the beneficiary is outside of the United States, they can apply for a visa at a US consulate or embassy abroad and then seek admission to the United States (see additional information below). If USCIS is not satisfied with the petition, it may also send a Request for Evidence (RFE). If the petition is denied, the employer and beneficiary have the option to appeal the decision or refile the petition with additional evidence. (See Chapter 7 for more information on Requests for Evidence).
- **Visa Application for Those Outside the US:** If the applicant is outside the United States, they must apply for an H-1B visa at a US consulate upon petition approval. However, if the applicant is from Canada or Bermuda, this step is not needed.
- **Entry and Claiming H-1B Status:** After obtaining the H-1B visa (or receiving the notice of approved petition in the case of Canadians and Bermudians), the applicant can enter the US and claim H-1B status.

Read More: https://www.uscis.gov/working-in-the-united-states/temporary-workers/h-1b-specialty-occupations-and-fashion-models/h-1b-electronic-registration-process

Required Forms and Documents

Forms:

- ETA 9035 Labor Condition Application (LCA): This form is required to ensure that employment conditions meet the necessary standards.
- Form I-129 Petition for a Nonimmigrant Worker: This is the main form used to petition for a nonimmigrant worker.
- Form I-907 Request for Premium Processing Service: This form is optional and only used if premium processing is desired.

Required Documents for Evidence:

- Employment Contract: Must be signed by both the employer and the employee.
- Evidence of Qualified Specialty Occupation: Documents such as a detailed job description, job circular, statement letters, etc. to establish the job as a specialty occupation.
- Educational Qualifications: Documentation of the employee's education and relevant qualifications.
- Licenses and Certifications: Any necessary attestations or certifications of the employee to support the application.
- Passport and Travel Documents: Old and new passports, visa stamps, I-94, and any other travel documents as required.
- Proof of Employer's Ability to Pay Salary: Employer's tax returns, audited financial statements, copies of contracts or invoices with customers, quarterly payroll

records, marketing documents, etc. to demonstrate the existence and financial viability of the employer.

- Additional Documents: Any other documents as the case may need.

Processing Times

- **Lottery Processing Time:** Results of the H-1B visa lottery are typically announced around March 31st every year. In some cases, a second lottery may be conducted by USCIS.
- **Processing Time:** After being selected in the lottery, the processing time varies based on factors such as USCIS workload and case complexity. Generally, it takes anywhere from two (2) to six (6) months for the approval process to be completed.
- **USCIS Premium Processing:** Applicants have the option to pay an additional fee for premium processing, which typically takes fifteen (15) days.
- **Case Preparation Time:** Should the employer or beneficiary choose to contract the services of an immigration lawyer to prepare the case, it usually takes two (2) to three (3) weeks after the approval of the LCA to put the application filing together, depending on the complexity and needs of the case.

Read more: https://www.uscis.gov/i-129

USCIS Fees

While processing the H-1B visa petition, several fees need to be submitted to USCIS, including:

- **Lottery Registration Fee:** For Cap-Subject applications, the petitioner needs to pay $215 for the Lottery Registration.
- **I-129 Filing Fee (H-1B Petition):** The primary fee required for submitting an H-1B petition (Form I-129) is the filing fee. As of the latest update, this fee stands at $460 for employers with one (1) to twenty-five (25) full-time employees and $780 for employers with twenty-six (26) or more full-time employees. This fee covers the basic processing costs associated with the H-1B petition.
- **ACWIA Fee:** The American Competitiveness and Workforce Improvement Act (ACWIA) fee is used to support educational and training initiatives in the US workforce. The ACWIA fee varies depending on the size of the employer—ranging from $750 for smaller employers to $1,500 for larger ones.
- **Asylum Program Fees (APF):** The employer needs to pay this fee which is $300 for employers with one (1) to twenty-five (25) full-time workers and $600 for those with twenty-six (26) or more full-time workers. Non-profit entities are exempt from this fee.
- **Fraud Prevention and Detection Fee:** To maintain the integrity of the H-1B program, a fraud prevention and detection fee of $500 is required. This fee supports efforts to prevent and investigate fraudulent activities related to H-1B visa petitions.
- **Public Law Fee:** Applicable to certain employers, the Public Law fee of $4,000 is levied on companies with over fifty (50) employees of which more than fifty (50)

percent are either H-1B or L-1 visa holders. This fee aims to incentivize companies to hire US workers and invest in workforce development programs.

- **Premium Processing Fee:** For those seeking expedited processing of their H-1B visa petition, a premium processing fee of $2,805 is available. This fee guarantees a response from USCIS within fifteen (15) calendar days, a significantly reduced processing time compared to standard processing.

It is important to check the latest fee schedule on the official website of USCIS, as fees may change over time.

For updated information, please check:

https://www.uscis.gov/forms/all-forms/h-and-l-filing-fees-for-form-i-129-petition-for-a-nonimmigrant-worker

2. Temporary Agricultural Workers: H-2A

What is an H-2A visa?

The H-2A program enables US employers or US agents who meet certain regulatory requirements to bring foreign nationals to the US to fill temporary agricultural jobs. A US employer, a US agent as described in the regulations, or an association of US agricultural producers named as a joint employer must file Form I-129, Petition for a Nonimmigrant Worker, on the prospective worker's behalf.

Those who plan to work in temporary or seasonal agricultural jobs are eligible for the H-2A visa. "Seasonal" refers to the fact that the work falls inside a predetermined time frame or occasion. "Temporary" refers to projects that are finished in less than one (1) year.

Who May Be Eligible for H-2A Status?

To be eligible for H-2A nonimmigrant status, the employer (petitioner) must meet the following requirements:

- Provide a job that is temporary or seasonal.
- Demonstrate that there are not enough US workers who are able, willing, qualified, and available to do the temporary work.
- Exemplify that hiring H-2A workers will not have a negative impact on the wages and working conditions of similarly employed US workers.
- Provide a single, valid temporary labor certification from the DOL with the I-129 petition. There is a limited exception to this requirement in certain "emergent circumstances."

H-2A Application Process

Step 1: The petitioner must apply for and obtain a temporary labor certification for H-2A workers from the DOL prior to asking USCIS for H-2A classification.

Step 2: After getting a temporary labor certification from the DOL for H-2A employment, the petitioner needs to submit Form I-129 to USCIS. With a few exceptions, the petitioner must include the original temporary labor certification with Form I-129 as the first piece of evidence.

Step 3: After USCIS approves Form I-129, prospective H-2A workers outside of the US must do one (1) of the following:

- Apply for an H-2A visa with the US Department of State (DOS) at a US embassy or consulate abroad and then apply for admission to the US with US Customs and Border Protection (CBP) at a US port of entry; or
- Directly seek admission to the US in H-2A classification with CBP at a US port of entry (in cases where an H-2A visa is not required).

Timeline

USCIS's processing times for H-2A petitions can vary. Employers can opt for premium processing to expedite the review of the I-129.

- Regular Processing Timeline: Approximately two (2) to three (3) months.
- Premium Processing Timeline: fifteen (15) calendar days.

How long does H-2A status last?

Generally, USCIS may grant H-2A classification for up to the period authorized on the temporary labor certification, with possible extensions in increments of up to one (1) year, each requiring a new, valid labor certification.

3. Nonimmigrant Trainee or Special Education Exchange Visitor: H-3

What is an H-3 visa?

The H-3 visa mostly comes into play when a US-based corporation has its establishment in a foreign location and wants to train employees at its training center in the US. This visa category also allows Special Education Exchange Visitors (SEEVs) to come temporarily and receive training in the US under the H-3 category.

In both cases, the purpose of the H-3 classification is *not* productive employment in the US. Instead, this visa type is specifically designed to allow foreign nationals to receive training that is unavailable in their home country or country of residence.

Who is eligible to apply for an H-3 visa?

- Trainees: These are foreign nationals who reside in a foreign country and are coming temporarily to the US as trainees. The trainee must have received an invitation from a US organization or person to receive training in any field including but not limited to agriculture, commerce, communications, finance, government, transportation, and other professions. Note: the allowed fields of training do not include graduate medical education or training.
- Special Education Exchange Visitors (SEEVs): These are foreign nationals who seek to participate in training programs dedicated to the education of children with physical, mental, or emotional disabilities. A Special Education Exchange Visitor must have a baccalaureate degree in special education (or be nearing the completion of a baccalaureate degree in the same) and have extensive prior training and experience in teaching children with physical, mental, or emotional disabilities.

What are the requirements for a program to be able to petition for an H-3 trainee?

The petition for an H-3 visa can only be filed by a US employer or organization (petitioner). When filing the petition, the petitioner must demonstrate that:

- The proposed training is not available in the trainee's country;
- The trainee will not be employed in the normal operation of the business and will not engage in productive employment that is not necessary for the training; and
- The training will benefit the trainee in pursuing a career outside the US.

Some characteristics of a training program that may render it incompatible with the H-3 visa program include but are not limited to:

- The program is incompatible with the practitioner's business or enterprise.
- The petitioner invites a trainee who already possesses substantial expertise and training in the proposed field of training.
- The proposed program is in a field of knowledge that is unlikely to be used outside the US.
- The petitioner does not have sufficiently trained staff in the US to train the trainee.
- The program intends to extend the total allowable period of practical training previously authorized to a nonimmigrant student.

Process of Filing an H-3 Petition for a Trainee

The petitioner needs to file an H-3 Petition for a Nonimmigrant Worker (Form I-129) with the USCIS together with supporting documents. The petition must contain a specific description of the training program that includes a) a description of the type of training and supervision to be given; b) reasons why such training cannot be obtained in the trainee's country; and c) indications as to the source of any remuneration to be received by the trainee as well as any benefit that will be accrued to the petitioner.

What are the requirements for a program to petition for an H-3 Special Education Exchange Visitor (SEEV)?

The petition must be filed by a facility with a structured program and trained staff that have the capability to provide education to children with disabilities as well as training to participants in the field of special education. Furthermore, any custodial care of children must be incidental to the beneficiary's training. Important note: In this particular subset of the H-3 program, there is a cap of fifty (50) visas per fiscal year.

Process of Filing an H-3 Petition for a Special Education Exchange Visitor (SEEV)

As in the case of Trainees, the US facility providing the training to the SEEV needs to file an H-3 Petition for a Nonimmigrant Worker (Form I-129). The petition must include a description of a) the training the applicant will receive; b) the qualifications of the professional staff at the facility; and c) the beneficiary's participation in the training program.

Family Members of H-3 Trainees and Special Education Exchange Visitors (SEEVs)

The spouse and unmarried children of an H-3 visa holder are allowed to accompany them to the US as H-4 nonimmigrants. However, family members are not permitted to work in the US during their stay.

Period of Stay for H-3 Visa Holders

H-3 Trainees are allowed to remain in the US for up to two (2) years. However, SEEVs are only allowed to remain in the US for a period of up to eighteen (18) months.

4. Religious Worker Visa: R-1

What is an R-1 visa?

R-1 is a nonimmigrant visa for foreign nationals who seek to work in the US temporarily in a religious occupation.

To be eligible for an R-1 visa, the foreign national has to be offered employment by one of the following:

1. A non-profit religious organization in the US,
2. A religious organization that is authorized by a group tax exemption holder to use its group tax exemption, or
3. A non-profit organization affiliated with a religious denomination(s) in the US.

There are three (3) types of religious workers who are eligible for R-1 status, given that they fulfill the other requirements:

1. Minister: Ministers of the denomination of the US-based employer
2. Religious vocation: Those who are in a religious vocation (such as nuns, monks, etc.)
3. Religious occupation: Those in another religious occupation (i.e., those who perform day-to-day work at a religious organization, such as missionaries, religious instructors, etc.)

Eligibility Criteria

Since the R-1 visa is for non-profit religious organization employees only, to be eligible, both the US employer and the foreign employee need to meet certain criteria.

Eligibility criteria for the foreign employee:

1. Two (2) years of continuous membership in any US-based religious organization immediately preceding the petition, and
2. Two (2) years of experience in any religious organization after the age of fourteen (14) and immediately preceding the petition.

The employee must also be coming to the US to work part-time or full-time (at least twenty (20) hours per week) at the organization as a religious worker.

Eligibility criteria for the US employer:

1. A non-profit religious organization, or
2. A part of a larger non-profit religious denomination.

To prove eligibility, both the employee and the employer must provide relevant documents as evidence (see complete list below).

Processing

First, the US employer (petitioner) needs to file Form I-129 with USCIS on the foreign employee's (beneficiary's) behalf. In addition, at the time of the petition, both the petitioner and the beneficiary will have to provide proof of eligibility for an R-1 visa.

The processing times of the R-1 petition can vary, and approval of the R-1 petition includes an on-site inspection by USCIS as one of its eligibility criteria. If this inspection has already been completed previously, the R-1 petition can qualify for premium processing, which is faster than regular processing and completed within fifteen (15) days. Regular processing of an R-1 petition can take up to eight (8) to nine (9) months. The fee for regular processing of the I-129 form for an R-1 at this time is $1,015, while the fee for premium processing is $1,685. Please refer to the USCIS website for current processing fees and times.

If USCIS finds that the documents provided satisfy its requirements, then the beneficiary will be granted R-1 status (if physically present in the US and eligible for a change of status). If the beneficiary is outside of the US, they will need to obtain an R-1 visa from a US consulate by submitting Form DS-160 and scheduling an interview. The time it takes for a visa to be issued can depend on a number of issues.

Petitioner and Beneficiary Requirements

1. Petitioner requirements:

a. A properly completed current version of the Petition for a Nonimmigrant Worker (Form I-129) along with the R-1 Classification Supplement

b. Evidence that the petitioner is either a bona fide non-profit religious organization or a bona fide organization that is affiliated with a religious denomination and is exempt from taxation.

To demonstrate tax exemption, the organization must submit evidence that:

- The organization is exempt from federal tax requirements as described in Section 501(c)(3) of the Internal Revenue Code (IRC) of 1986
- The organization has a currently valid determination letter from the Internal Revenue Service (IRS) confirming such exemption.

If the petitioning entity falls under a group tax exemption, it must provide evidence such as:

- A letter from the organization holding the group exemption as evidence that the petitioner is covered by such exemption;
- Copies of pages from a directory for the parent organization showing the petitioner as a member of the group;
- The parent organization's website that lists the petitioner as a member of the group covered by the exemption; or

- An IRS letter confirming the petitioner's coverage under the parent organization exemption.

c. Verifiable evidence of how the petitioner intends to compensate the beneficiary, including whether or not the beneficiary will be self-supporting. For this, the following forms of evidence are acceptable:
  - Documentation of past compensation for similar positions;
  - Budgets showing monies set aside for salaries, leases, etc.;
  - Documentary evidence demonstrating that room and board will be provided; or
  - Other evidence acceptable to USCIS.

In the case of a self-supporting beneficiary, the petitioner must provide:

- Evidence demonstrating that the petitioner has an established program

For temporary, uncompensated missionary work;

- Evidence demonstrating that the denomination maintains missionary programs both in the United States and abroad;
- Evidence of the beneficiary's acceptance into the missionary program;
- Evidence demonstrating the religious duties and responsibilities associated with traditionally uncompensated missionary work; and
- Copies of the beneficiary's bank records and budgets documenting the sources of self-support.

2. Beneficiary Requirements

a. To qualify for R-1 classification, the beneficiary must:

- Be a member of a religious denomination having a bona fide non-profit religious organization in the United States for at least the two (2) years immediately preceding the filing of the petition;
- Be coming to the United States to work in at least a part-time position (at least twenty (20) hours per week);
- Be coming solely as a minister or to perform a religious vocation or occupation role;
- Be coming to or remaining in the United States at the request of the petitioner to work solely for the petitioner; and
- Not intend to work in the United States in any capacity not included in a DHS-approved petition.

Evidence and Supporting Documents

The petitioner must submit the following evidence to establish that the beneficiary meets the requirements for R-1 nonimmigrant classification.

Ministers

For ministers, the petitioner must submit the following:

- A copy of the beneficiary's certificate of ordination or similar documents;
- Documents reflecting acceptance of the beneficiary's qualifications as a minister in the religious denomination; and

- Evidence that the beneficiary has completed any course of prescribed theological education at an accredited theological institution normally required or recognized by that religious denomination, including transcripts, curriculum, and documentation that establishes that the theological education is accredited by the denomination.

For denominations that do not require a theological education, the petitioner must instead submit evidence of:

- The denomination's requirements for ordination to minister;
- Duties allowed to be performed under ordination;
- The denomination's levels of ordination, if any; and
- The beneficiary's completion of the denomination's requirements for ordination.

Religious Vocations and Occupations

For a beneficiary who will work in a religious vocation or occupation, the petitioner must submit evidence of the following:

- The beneficiary is entering the United States to perform a religious vocation or occupation, as defined above (in either a professional or nonprofessional capacity)
- The beneficiary is qualified for the religious occupation or vocation according to the denomination's standards

All Beneficiaries
- The beneficiary's tax returns in the US, if applicable
- Valid passport with visa stamps
- One photograph in compliance with US visa photo requirements
- Form I-94

Period of Stay
1. USCIS grants R-1 status for an initial period of admission for up to thirty (30) months and subsequent extensions for up to an additional thirty (30) months.
2. The total period one can stay in the US under the R-1 visa cannot exceed five (5) years or sixty (60) months.
3. Foreign employees may apply for a new R-1 visa with a new five-year maximum stay, however, to be eligible for this, the applicant must have been physically present outside the US for the immediate previous year.

5. Exchange Visitor Visa: J-1 Waiver and Implications for Employers

What is a J-1 visa?
J-1 is a nonimmigrant visa category that allows individuals to participate in work and study-based exchange visitor programs in the United States. Applicants in this category must be sponsored by an exchange program that is designated as such by the US Department of State.

This visa category includes but not limited to:

- Professors
- Research scholars
- Short-term scholars
- Students: degree-seeking (bachelor, master, doctoral), non-degree seeking, and interns

Key Features

Categories: The J-1 visa includes categories such as au pairs, interns, trainees, scholars, researchers, and specialists.

Duration: The length of stay depends on the specific J-1 category, ranging from a few months to several years.

Sponsorship: Applicants must be sponsored by a designated program authorized by the US Department of State.

Two-Year Home-Country Physical Presence Requirement

Certain J-1 exchange visitors are subjected to a two-year home-country physical presence requirement. This means that, after the completion of the program, J-1 visitors are required to return to their home country or country of last legal residence for at least two (2) years. This requirement is part of the US Immigration and Nationality Act, Section 212(e). However, under certain conditions, this requirement can be waived (see below).

Waiver of the Two-Year Home Residency Requirement

J-1 exchange visitors subject to the two-year home-country residency requirement who are unable or unwilling to return to and remain in their home country or country of last legal residence for the required two (2) years may be able to obtain a J-1 waiver from the Department of Homeland Security (DHS) and US Citizenship and Immigration Services (USCIS). If the waiver is granted, the J-1 could change their status to another nonimmigrant status or adjust their status to US permanent resident if they can qualify for another nonimmigrant or immigrant visa category (for example, begin an H-1B employment position) without the need to remain outside the US for two (2) years.

Basis for Recommendation of a Waiver

J-1 exchange visitors who wish to obtain a J-1 waiver must apply to the Department of State's Waiver Review Division for a recommendation that USCIS grant a waiver. They can request a waiver under any one (1) of the five (5) bases in US immigration law, which are as follows:

1. **No Objection Statement.** No Objection Statement is the most commonly used of the five (5) bases. In this particular base, J-1 exchange visitors must obtain a No Objection Statement from their home country or country of last legal residence. The document states that the home country or country of last legal residence has no objection to the J-1 exchange visitor not returning and satisfying the two-year home-country physical presence requirement and also has no objection to the possibility of the J-1 exchange visitor becoming a lawful permanent resident of the United States.

2. **Request by an Interested US Federal Government Agency.** If a J-1 exchange visitor is working on a project for or of interest to a US federal government agency, and that agency determines that the individual's two-year absence would delay or be detrimental to the project, then that agency may request an Interested Government Agency Waiver on the individual's behalf. A list of federal agencies and designated officials can be found on the State Department's website.

3. **Persecution.** J-1 exchange visitors who believe that, upon returning to their home country, they could be persecuted based on their race, religion, or political beliefs may apply for a J-1 waiver on the base of persecution.

4. **Exceptional Hardship to a US Citizen (or Lawful Permanent Resident) Spouse or Child.** If a J-1 exchange visitor can show that their departure from the US would cause exceptional hardship to their US citizen or Lawful Permanent Resident spouse and/or child, they may apply for a waiver under this base. Mere separation from a family member does not count as "exceptional hardship" in this situation.

5. **Request by a Designated State Public Health Department or Its Equivalent (Conrad State 30 Program).** J-1 exchange visitors who are foreign medical graduates pursuing graduate medical training or education may apply for a waiver based on the request of a designated State Public Health Department or its equivalent, also known as the

Conrad State 30 Program. They must fulfill the following criteria if they want to obtain the waiver under this base:

- Have an offer of full-time employment at a healthcare facility in a designated healthcare professional shortage area or at a healthcare facility that serves patients from such a designated area;
- Agree to begin employment at that facility within ninety (90) days of receiving a J-1 waiver; and
- Sign a contract to continue working at that healthcare facility for a total of forty (40) hours per week and not less than three (3) years.

Each US state has a listing of Designated State Public Health Departments, which can be found on the US State Department website (travel.state.gov). Each health department can request up to thirty (30) J-1 waivers per federal fiscal year. Ten (10) out of the thirty (30) requests may be for J-1 physicians who will serve at facilities not located in a designated health care professional shortage area, but which serve patients who live in a designated area.

Application Process

1. The waiver applicant submits Form DS-3035, J-1 Visa Waiver Recommendation Application, to the Department of State.
2. The application is reviewed, and if the waiver is granted, the applicant may remain in the US to pursue a change or adjustment of status without needing to fulfill the two-year home residency requirement.

Implications for Employers

Sponsorship Responsibilities: Employers who sponsor J-1 visa holders must ensure compliance with the regulations of the Department of State and the specific J-1 program requirements. This includes providing appropriate training or internship opportunities and maintaining records of the J-1 participant's activities.

Compliance with Program Regulations: Employers must adhere to the terms of the J-1 exchange program, including the educational or training objectives outlined in the program. Failure to comply can result in penalties for both the employer and the J-1 participant.

Impact of the Two-Year Home Residency Requirement: Employers need to be aware that J-1 visa holders subject to the two-year home residency requirement may face restrictions on their ability to change status or apply for certain visas or permanent residency if they do not either fulfill the requirement or obtain a waiver. This can affect long-term employment plans and may require employers to consider alternative visa options for the employee.

Potential for Waiver Requests: Employers should be prepared to support J-1 visa holders who wish to seek waivers of the two-year home residency requirement. Providing documentation and justifications for the employee's waiver request may be necessary, particularly if the waiver is requested based on national interest or exceptional hardship.

Impact on Recruitment and Retention: The requirement for J-1 visa holders to return to their home country may impact recruitment and retention strategies. Employers should consider the implications for workforce stability and plan accordingly if key employees are subject to this requirement.

6. Visa for Athletes: P-1A

What is a P-1A visa?

P-1A is a nonimmigrant visa category designed for athletes who wish to enter the United States temporarily to participate in a specific athletic competition. This classification is specifically tailored to accommodate various types of athletes, ranging from individual competitors to members of professional teams.

Eligibility Criteria

An athlete who falls into one of the following categories and who intends to enter the United States temporarily solely for the purpose of performing at a specific athletic competition is eligible for a P-1A visa.

Internationally Recognized Individual Athletes

This category is for individual athletes who are internationally recognized for their high level of achievement in a particular sport.

The athlete must be coming to the US to compete in a specific event that is renowned and requires participation from athletes who have international recognition. The athlete's achievement must be significantly above average, with recognition in more than one (1) country.

Internationally Recognized Athletic Teams

This applies to athletes who are part of a team that is recognized internationally for its accomplishments in a particular sport.

The team must be competing in an event that is distinguished and recognized internationally. The event should require the participation of teams that have achieved international recognition.

Professional Athletes

This category is for athletes employed by a US-based team or franchise.

The team must be a member of an association that includes at least six (6) professional sports teams, with combined revenue of more than $10 million annually. The association must regulate its members and govern the competitions they participate in.

Alternatively, the athlete can be employed by a minor league team affiliated with such an association.

Amateur Athletes or Coaches

This applies to athletes or coaches who are part of a team or franchise in the US that belongs to a foreign league or association.

- The foreign league or association must consist of at least fifteen (15) amateur sports teams.
- Participation in the league must render players ineligible, temporarily or permanently, to receive

scholarships or participate in the sport at a US college or university under NCAA rules.

- The league must represent the highest level of amateur performance for that sport in the relevant foreign country, and a significant number of its players must typically be drafted by major or minor league sports teams in the US.

Theatrical Ice Skaters

This category is for professional or amateur ice skaters.

The athlete must be coming to the US to participate in a specific theatrical ice skating production or tour, either as an individual performer or as part of a group.

Who can file a P-1A petition?

For a P-1A visa, a US employer, agent, or sponsor plays the role of the petitioner in the application process. Here's how each of these entities is involved:

US Employer

A US employer can file a petition for an athlete seeking a P-1A visa. This is common for athletes who are being hired to compete or perform for a specific team, franchise, or organization based in the United States.

US Agent

A US agent can act as the petitioner for a P-1A visa, especially in situations where the athlete will be working for multiple employers or participating in various events. An agent may represent an individual athlete or a team.

US Sponsor

A US sponsor, such as an athletic organization, league, or sports association, can also petition for an athlete under the P-1A visa category. Sponsors are typically organizations that have a vested interest in the athlete's participation in a specific event or competition.

Application Process

The general steps involved in the P-1A visa process are:

Filing the Petition: The petitioning US employer, agent, or sponsor must submit Form I-129 to USCIS, along with the necessary supporting documentation (see below).

Supporting Documentation: This includes proof of the athlete's international recognition, the nature of the competition, the athlete's achievements, and contracts or agreements outlining the athlete's role.

Petition Approval and Visa Issuance: Once USCIS approves the petition, the athlete can apply for a P-1A visa at a US embassy or consulate. If already in the US with another valid immigration status, the athlete may be able to change their status to P-1A without the necessity of leaving the US to apply for a P-1A visa abroad.

Period of Stay

- The initial period of stay for an **individual athlete** is granted for up to five (5) years, depending on the time needed to complete the event, competition, or performance for which the visa was issued. Should the athlete need additional time to continue or finalize their activities, they can apply for an extension of stay in increments of up to five (5) years with a total stay limit of ten (10) years.

- The initial period of stay for an **athletic group** is granted for up to one (1) year, depending on the time needed to complete the event, competition, or performance for which the visa was issued. Should the athletic group need additional time to continue or finalize their activities, they can apply for an extension of stay in increments of up to one (1) year.
- To apply for an extension, a new Form I-129 must be filed with USCIS. This form can also be used for changing status, extending stay, or changing employment. This flexibility helps ensure that individual athletes and teams can complete their events, competitions, or performances in the US without interruption.

7. Members of Internationally Recognized Entertainment Groups: P-1B

What is a P-1B visa?

P-1B is a nonimmigrant visa category designed for individuals who are part of an entertainment group that has achieved international recognition. This classification is specifically for those who wish to enter the United States temporarily to perform as a member of such a group. The group must be well-established and recognized as outstanding in its field and must have maintained this recognition for a significant period.

Eligibility Criteria:

To qualify for the P-1B visa, the following conditions must be met:

Group's Recognition and Establishment:

- The entertainment group must have been established for at least one (1) year.
- The group must be internationally recognized, with a high level of achievement in its field, evidenced by skill and recognition that is significantly above average. The group's achievement should be renowned or well-known in more than one (1) country.
- The reputation of the group as a whole, rather than the individual achievements of its members, is the primary criterion for eligibility.

Membership Consistency:

- At least seventy-five (75) percent of the members of the group must have been a part of the group for at least one (1) year, demonstrating the group's cohesion and a sustained relationship between its members.

Exclusion of Individual Entertainers:

- Individual entertainers who are not performing as part of a group are not eligible for the P-1B visa classification. This visa is strictly for members of an entertainment group.

Special Provisions for Certain Groups:

Circus Performers and Essential Circus Personnel:

> Circus performers and essential circus personnel are exempt from the one-year membership and international group recognition requirements. However, the circus must at least be nationally recognized.

Nationally Recognized Entertainment Groups:

> Some other entertainment groups that are recognized nationally but not internationally may also have the international recognition requirement waived. To qualify for this waiver, the group must demonstrate that it has been recognized as outstanding in its field nationally for a sustained period and that other special circumstances exist to justify the waiver.

Who can file a P-1B petition?

For the P-1B visa, the petition must be filed by a US employer, a US sponsoring organization, a US agent, or a foreign employer through a US agent. Here's an overview of each of these roles:

US Employer

A US employer is a company or organization based in the United States that will employ the entertainment group. This employer is directly responsible for filing the petition on behalf of the group members.

US Sponsoring Organization

A US sponsoring organization is an entity that will sponsor the entertainment group for performances or events in the United States. This can be a production company, an event organizer, or any other organization that has a vested interest in bringing the group to the US for specific activities.

US Agent

A US agent can file the P-1B petition on behalf of the entertainment group, especially when the group will be performing for multiple employers or participating in various events across the country. An agent can represent the entire group or individual members within the group.

Foreign Employer through a US Agent

A foreign employer can also file a P-1B petition for an entertainment group, but this must be done through a US agent. The foreign employer remains the direct employer of the group, but the US agent acts as the petitioner on the foreign employer's behalf.

Petition Procedure

To obtain a P-1B visa, a petition must be filed with USCIS by a US employer, US sponsoring organization, US agent, or a foreign employer through a US agent. The petition process includes the following steps:

Prepare Form I-129:

Form I-129 must be completed by the petitioner.

- o If acting as an agent for multiple employers, the petitioner must prove their authority to represent all the employers involved.

Gather Supporting Documentation:

Labor Organization Consultation: A written consultation from a relevant labor organization or proof that the group has been established and performing for at least one (1) year.

Itinerary: A detailed schedule of performances with dates and locations.

Contracts/Agreements: A copy of the contract or a summary of the terms of the employment agreement.

Group's Establishment Evidence: Proof that the group has been performing regularly for at least one (1) year.

Proof of International Recognition:

Significant Awards/Nominations: Evidence of the group's receipt of or nomination for international awards.

Additional Evidence (three (3) required): Documentation showing the group's leading performances, international acclaim, commercial success, recognition from experts, or high remuneration.

Submit Petition:

- The completed petition with all supporting documents and corresponding filing fee must be submitted to USCIS.

- Once approved, the group members can apply for a P-1B visa at a US embassy or consulate.

Period of Stay

Under the P-1B visa, entertainment group members are granted an initial period of stay of up to one (1) year to complete the event, competition, or performance for which the visa was issued. Should the group need additional time to continue or finalize their activities, they can apply for an extension of stay. Extensions can be granted in increments of up to one (1) year, allowing for the completion of ongoing engagements.

To apply for an extension, a new Form I-129 must be filed with USCIS. This form can also be used for changing status, extending stay, or changing employment. This flexibility helps ensure that entertainment groups can complete their engagements in the US without interruption.

8. Individual Performer or Part of a Group Performing Under a Reciprocal Exchange Program: P-2

What is a P-2 visa?

A P-2 visa allows foreign artists or entertainers to enter the United States temporarily to perform as part of a reciprocal exchange program between a US organization and a foreign organization. This visa was created to foster international cultural and artistic collaboration.

Eligibility Criteria:

Reciprocal Exchange Program:

- o The performer must be coming to the US through a government-recognized reciprocal exchange program. Currently, there are five (5) specific P-2 reciprocal agreements in place:
  - The American Federation of Musicians (US) and the American Federation of Musicians (Canada).
  - Actor's Equity Association (US) and the Canadian Actors' Equity Association.
  - Actor's Equity Association (US) and the British Actors' Equity Association.
  - The International Council of Air Shows and the Canadian Air Show Association.
  - The Alliance of Canadian Cinema Television and Radio Artists (ACTRA) and the Screen Actors Guild/American Federation of Television and Radio Artists (SAG-AFTRA).
- o If a reciprocal agreement not listed above is submitted, USCIS will review it to ensure it meets the regulatory standards.

Comparable Skills:

- The performer must possess skills that are comparable to those of US artists and entertainers participating in the exchange program outside the United States. This ensures that the exchange maintains a high standard of artistic and professional quality.

Who can file a P-2 visa petition?

To qualify for a P-2 visa, a Petition for a Nonimmigrant Worker (Form I-129), must be filed on the foreign performer's behalf by either a sponsoring labor organization or a US employer. Here's an overview of the roles and responsibilities of each of these entities:

Sponsoring Labor Organization:

- This is an organization in the US that represents artists or entertainers in a specific field or industry. The labor organization must be recognized as representing the interests of performers within the exchange program's scope. They are responsible for ensuring that the exchange adheres to the program's standards and that the performers are appropriately represented.

US Employer:

- The US employer is an individual or organization that is directly hiring the foreign artist or entertainer for a specific performance or series of performances under the reciprocal exchange program. The employer must be actively involved in the performance or engagement and capable of fulfilling the terms of the program.

Application Procedure

The application process for a P-2 visa involves the following steps:

Complete Form I-129:

- The sponsoring labor organization in the United States or the US employer must complete Form I-129, Petition for a Nonimmigrant Worker, on the foreign national's behalf.
- If the petitioner is acting as an agent for multiple employers, they must prove their authorization to represent all involved parties.

Gather Required Supporting Documents:

Written Consultation: A consultation from an appropriate labor organization.

Reciprocal Exchange Agreement: A copy of the formal agreement between the US sponsoring organization and the foreign organization receiving the reciprocal US artist or entertainer.

Reciprocal Exchange Description: A statement from the sponsoring organization describing the reciprocal nature of the exchange.

Comparable Skills Evidence: Proof that the skills of the US artist or entertainer and the foreign artist or entertainer are comparable and that the terms of employment are similar.

Labor Organization Involvement: Evidence that an appropriate US labor organization was involved in negotiating the terms or has endorsed the reciprocal exchange.

Itinerary: If the events or performances occur in multiple locations, an itinerary listing the dates and locations of these events must be provided.

Submit Petition:

- The completed petition with all supporting documents and corresponding filing fee must be submitted to USCIS.
- Once approved, the foreign performer can apply for a P-2 visa at a US embassy or consulate and enter the US in P-2 status.

Period of Stay

Under the P-2 visa, the initial period of stay allows for up to one (1) year to complete a specific event, competition, or performance. If additional time is required to continue or finalize these activities, an extension can be granted in increments of up to one (1) year. This provision provides the necessary flexibility for artists and entertainers to fulfill their commitments under the reciprocal exchange program, ensuring they have adequate time to complete their engagements in the United States.

9. Artists or Entertainers in Culturally Unique Programs: P-3

What is a P-3 visa?

A P-3 visa is a temporary work visa for foreign artists and entertainers coming to the US to be part of a culturally unique program. The applicant's role can be to perform, teach, or coach as an artist or entertainer. Such programs can be either commercially motivated or not commercially motivated.

This visa may be granted to either an individual or a group. The visa holder may be admitted to the US for an initial period of up to one (1) year, and this time can be extended upon application in increments of not more than one (1) year.

Eligibility Criteria for P-3 Visa

An applicant needs to meet the following eligibility criteria to be granted a P-3 visa:

- The purpose of visiting the US should be to develop, interpret, represent, coach, or teach at a unique or traditional ethnic, folk, cultural, musical, theatrical, or performance event.
- The applicant must be sponsored by an organization or agent in the US.
- Applicants must be in good health and have good moral character.
- A Petition for Nonimmigrant Worker (Form I-129) must be filed by the US employer or agent.
- Every presentation and event should be culturally distinct.

P-3 Visa Important Facts

- Applicants may legally work in the US only for their P-3 sponsor. To change jobs, workers must apply for a change of status or obtain a new visa.
- P-3 visas are readily available.
- P-3 visas will be issued for the duration necessary to complete a specific event, tour, or season, with a maximum length of one (1) year.

- As long as the visa stamp and status are valid, a P-3 visa holder may travel in and out of the US or remain in the US continuously.

Can a P-3 Visa be Extended?

Under the conditions of the P-3 visa, beneficiaries are only allowed to remain in the US for the duration of the cultural event, activity, or performance—not to exceed one (1) calendar year. However, in some cases, an extension of stay may be authorized by USCIS in increments of one (1) year to enable P-3 visa holders to continue or finish the same event or activity for which the status was granted.

If a P-3 visa holder wishes to remain in the US for longer than one (1) additional year, they may need to change their nonimmigrant status to a different type that would allow for a longer stay. Alternatively, the individual may also wish to seek a new visa under another employer.

A P-3 can apply to change their nonimmigrant status as long as they meet the following criteria:

- Were lawfully admitted to the US under a nonimmigrant visa
- Still have valid nonimmigrant status
- Have not violated any of the conditions of their status
- Have not committed any crimes during their stay

Can a Family Member of a P-3 Visa Holder Come to the US?

P-3 visa holders are permitted to bring their spouse and unmarried children under the age of twenty-one (21) with them to the US. Other family members such as parents, grandparents, or in-laws are not eligible for this privilege.

Eligible family members must obtain a P-4 visa to travel to the US. P-4 visas can be requested at the same time as the P-3 visa. Family members will need to attend the visa interview together with the principal P-3 applicant.

10. Individuals with Extraordinary Ability or Achievement: O-1

What is an O-1 visa?

An O-1 visa is a nonimmigrant work visa for individuals with extraordinary abilities in the sciences, arts, education, business, or athletics, or for individuals with a record of extraordinary achievement in the motion picture or television industry. This visa category recognizes those who have been nationally or internationally acknowledged for their exceptional talents.

The O-1 visa classification is divided into two (2) main subsets:

1. **O-1A:** For individuals with extraordinary ability in the sciences, education, business, or athletics (excluding the arts, motion picture, or television industry).
2. **O-1B:** For individuals with extraordinary ability in the arts (O-1B Arts) or extraordinary achievement in the motion picture or television industry (O-1B MPTV).

Eligibility Criteria for an O-1 Visa Employee

To qualify for an O-1 visa, an employee must meet the following criteria:

1. Demonstrated Extraordinary Ability:

- **O-1A:** Must show sustained national or international acclaim and recognition in their field, indicating they are among the top few percent who have reached the peak of their discipline.
- **O-1B (Arts):** Must show a high level of achievement in the arts, characterized by prominence and recognition well above the norm.
- **O-1B (MPTV):** Must show a very high level of accomplishment in the motion picture or television industry, with substantial recognition in their field.

2. **Temporary Purpose of Visit:** Must be coming to the US temporarily to continue working in their area of extraordinary ability.

3. **Substantial Evidence:** Must provide substantial documentation of their extraordinary abilities or achievements, including awards, media coverage, memberships in elite organizations, or other evidence of significant contributions to their field as detailed below for each subset:

4. O-1A:

- **Prizes or Awards:** Documentation of nationally or internationally recognized prizes or awards for excellence.

- **Association Memberships:** Memberships in associations requiring outstanding achievements judged by recognized experts.
- **Published Material:** Articles or media coverage about the individual's work.
- **Judging of Others:** Evidence of judging the work of others in the field.
- **Original Contributions:** Evidence of significant original contributions to the field.
- **Authorship:** Scholarly articles in professional journals or major media.
- **Critical Employment:** Employment in essential roles for distinguished organizations.
- **High Salary:** Evidence of commanding a high salary or substantial remuneration.

O-1B (Arts):

- **Lead or Starring Roles:** Evidence of lead or starring roles in distinguished productions.
- **National or International Recognition:** Critical reviews or published materials about the individual.
- **Critical Roles in Esteemed Organizations:** Evidence of significant roles in renowned organizations.
- **Commercial or Critical Success:** Record of major successes, including box office receipts and ratings.
- **Significant Recognition:** Recognition from organizations, critics, or experts.
- **High Salary:** Evidence of commanding a high salary or substantial remuneration.

O-1B (MPTV):

- **Extraordinary Achievement:** Demonstrated record of extraordinary achievement in motion picture or television productions.
- **Recognition:** Recognition in the field through extensive documentation.

Eligibility Criteria for an O-1 Visa Employer

The eligibility criteria for the entities that can file an O-1 petition—namely, a US employer, a US agent, or a foreign employer through a US agent—vary depending on the role each plays in the petition process:

1. US Employer

The US employer must be a legitimate business or organization operating in the US that requires the services of a foreign national with extraordinary ability. The employer must provide a bona fide job offer for the beneficiary.

2. US Agent

A US agent can be an individual or a business entity that has the authority to act on behalf of the beneficiary and the employer(s). The agent must have a valid contractual relationship with the beneficiary or the employers.

The US agent can file the petition in three (3) capacities:

- **As an** Employer: If the agent is directly employing the beneficiary.
- As a Representative: If the agent represents both the beneficiary and multiple employers. In this case, the representative must provide a complete itinerary of

events and activities, along with contracts between the employers and the beneficiary.

- As a Foreign Employer's Agent: If acting on behalf of a foreign employer, the agent must demonstrate that they have the authority to act on behalf of the foreign employer in matters related to the petition.

3. Foreign Employer Through a US Agent

A foreign employer, which is a company or organization based outside of the US, can file an O-1 petition on behalf of the beneficiary through a US agent. The foreign employer must have a legitimate need for the beneficiary's services in the US but cannot directly file the petition with USCIS.

Application Process for an O-1 Visa

A US employer, US agent, or foreign employer through a US agent must file Form I-129, Petition for Nonimmigrant Worker, on behalf of the applicant. This petition should be filed no more than one (1) year before the services are needed and at least forty-five (45) days before the employment start date to avoid delays.

The petition must include:

- Consultation: A written advisory opinion from a peer group, labor organization, or management organization in the applicant's area of ability.
- Contract: A copy of any written contract between the petitioner and the beneficiary or a summary of the terms of the oral agreement.
- Itineraries: An explanation of the nature of the events or activities and a schedule of engagements.

- Evidence of O-1 Eligibility: Documentation proving the beneficiary's extraordinary ability or achievements.

Period of Stay and Extensions

Initial Period of Stay: Up to three (3) years, based on the time required to accomplish the event or activity.

Extension of Stay: May be granted in one-year increments to continue or complete the same event or activity. Extensions require Form I-129, a copy of Form I-94, and a statement explaining the necessity for the extension.

Changing Employers

If an O-1 visa holder wants to change employers, the new employer must file a new Form I-129. If an agent filed the original petition, the new employer must file an amended petition with evidence of the new employment arrangement and request for an extension of stay.

Material Changes in Employment

Any significant changes in the terms and conditions of employment require an amended Form I-129 to be filed with the USCIS Service Center that processed the original petition.

Return Transportation

If an O-1 visa holder's employment is terminated for reasons other than voluntary resignation, the employer must pay a reasonable amount for return transportation to the foreign national's last place of residence before entering the US. If an agent filed the petition, both the agent and employer share this responsibility.

Family of O-1 Visa Holders

Spouses and children under the age of twenty-one (21) accompanying or joining an O-1 visa holder at a later time (called "following to join") may be eligible to apply for an O-3 nonimmigrant visa. The O-3 visa is subject to the same period of admission and limitations as the primary O-1 visa holder. O-3 visa holders may not work in the United States under this classification but may engage in full or part-time study.

11. Essential Support Personnel for an O-1 Visa Holder: O-2

What is an O-2 visa?

O-2 is a nonimmigrant visa category designed for individuals who will accompany and assist an O-1 visa holder—typically an artist or athlete—in the performance of a specific event or activity. The O-2 visa holder's role must be essential to the O-1 visa holder's performance, and the O-2's skills must be unique and not readily available among US workers.

Eligibility Criteria for an O-2 Visa

Essential Support: The O-2 visa applicant must demonstrate that their assistance is essential to the successful performance of the O-1 visa holder. Their role should be integral to the O-1's work and not easily performed by a US worker.

Same Activity: The O-2 visa holder must accompany the O-1 visa holder to assist in the same event or activity. The assistance provided should be specialized—requiring specific skills, experience, or knowledge that the O-1 visa holder relies upon.

Visa Linkage: The O-2 visa is directly tied to the O-1 visa, meaning that it cannot exist independently. The O-2 visa is only valid as long as the O-1 visa holder remains engaged in the activity for which the visa was issued.

Who can file an O-2 petition?

An O-2 petition can be filed by the following entities:

US Employer:

- A US employer who is employing an O-1 visa holder can file a petition for an O-2 visa on behalf of the individual who will provide essential support to the O-1 visa holder.
- The employer must demonstrate that the O-2 beneficiary's role is crucial to the success of the O-1 visa holder's work.

US Agent:

- A US agent can file the petition on behalf of the O-2 visa applicant if the O-1 visa holder is working for multiple employers, or if the O-1 and O-2 visa holders are working as freelancers or on a project basis.
- The agent must provide an itinerary or schedule that outlines the O-1 and O-2 visa holders' engagements as well as prove that the O-2 visa holder's services are essential to the O-1 visa holder's activities.

Foreign Employer through a US Agent:

- If the O-1 visa holder is employed by a foreign employer, that employer can file an O-2 visa petition through a US agent. The US agent acts on behalf of the foreign employer to file the petition with US Citizenship and Immigration Services (USCIS).
- The US agent must demonstrate that the O-2 visa holder's role is indispensable to the success of the O-1 visa holder's activities in the US.

Petition Process for an O-2 Visa

Form I-129:

- A US employer or agent must complete and file Form I-129, Petition for a Nonimmigrant Worker, on the O-2 beneficiary's behalf with USCIS. This form must be accompanied by the required supporting documentation (see below), and both the O-1 and O-2 beneficiaries must have their own, separate Form I-129.
- The employer or agent cannot file the Form I-129 more than one (1) year before the O-1 visa holder is set to begin employment. However, to avoid delays, it is recommended that the petition be filed at least forty-five (45) days before the intended start date of employment.

Supporting Documentation:

Consultation: If the O-2 visa is sought to support an individual with extraordinary ability in athletics or the arts, a consultation letter from the appropriate labor organization is required. For those supporting an individual with extraordinary achievement in motion pictures or television, the consultation must come from both an appropriate labor organization and a management organization with expertise in the relevant skill area.

Evidence of Eligibility: The petitioner must submit evidence demonstrating the O-2 applicant's essentiality, critical skills, and experience working with the O-1 beneficiary. This includes proof of substantial experience in performing the critical skills and providing essential support services.

For motion picture or television production, the evidence should establish that significant production has taken place both in and outside the United States and that the O-2 visa holder's continuing participation is essential to the successful completion of the production.

Period of Stay and Extension of Stay

Initial Period of Stay: The O-2 visa is typically granted for up to three (3) years, depending on the time required to accomplish the event or activity.

Extension of Stay: Extensions are granted in increments of up to one (1) year, based on the time needed to continue or complete the same event or activity.

Upon arrival, O-2 visa holders may be admitted to the United States by DHS for the entire validity period of the petition plus up to an additional ten (10) days before the validity period begins and ten (10) days after it ends. However, note that O-2 visa holders are only authorized to work during the validity period of the petition.

Family of O-2 Visa Holders

O-3 Visa for Dependents: The spouse and unmarried children under the age of twenty-one (21) of an O-2 visa holder may accompany or join the O-2 visa holder in the United States under the O-3 nonimmigrant visa classification. O-3 visa holders are subject to the same period of admission and limitations as the O-2 visa holder.

Restrictions on Employment: O-3 visa holders are not permitted to work in the United States, however, they may engage in full-time or part-time study while in the US.

12. Intracompany Transferee—Executive or Manager: L-1A

What is an L-1A visa?

The L-1A visa was designed to enable US employers to transfer executives or managers from their foreign offices to their US offices. This visa also allows foreign companies that do not have an established US presence to send an executive or manager to the United States to set up a new office.

Dual Intention of an L-1A Visa

The L-1A visa is a "dual intent" visa, meaning that the visa holder can legally pursue permanent residency (a green card) in the United States while maintaining their L-1A nonimmigrant status. This is unlike many other nonimmigrant visas that require the holder to prove they do not intend to immigrate permanently to the US.

Dual intent allows L-1A visa holders to start the green card process through employment-based categories, such as the EB-1C for multinational managers and executives, without the need to leave the US or risk visa denial based on immigrant intent. This dual intent feature makes the L-1A visa particularly attractive for multinational companies and their executives or managers looking to establish long-term residency in the US.

Eligibility of the US Employer (Petitioner)

To be able to petition for an L-1A employee, the US employer must meet the following criteria:

Qualifying Relationship: The US employer must have a qualifying relationship with the foreign company. This relationship can be as a parent company, branch, subsidiary, or affiliate—collectively referred to as "qualifying organizations."

Business Operations: The US employer must be, or will be, actively doing business as an employer in the United States and at least one (1) other country. This business must be regular, systematic, and continuous and involve the provision of goods and/or services. The mere physical presence of an office or agent does not satisfy this requirement; the business must be viable and operational.

New Office Setup: For employers seeking to transfer foreign executives or managers to establish a new office in the US:

Physical Premises: The employer must have secured sufficient physical premises to house the new office.

Viability of US Office: The intended US office must be able to support an executive or managerial position within one (1) year of the petition's approval.

Employment History: The employer must have employed the beneficiary as an executive or manager for one (1) continuous year in the three (3) years preceding the filing of the petition.

Eligibility of L-1A Employee (Beneficiary)

To qualify for an L-1A visa, the foreign employee must meet the following conditions:

Work History: The employee must have been employed by the qualifying foreign organization for one (1) continuous year within the three (3) years immediately preceding their admission to the United States.

Position in the US: The employee must be entering the United States to work in an executive or managerial capacity for a branch of the same employer or one of its qualifying organizations (see descriptions below).

Executive Capacity: Refers to the ability to make decisions of wide latitude without much oversight.

Managerial Capacity: Refers to the ability to supervise and control the work of professional employees or manage the organization or a specific department, function, or component. It also includes the ability to manage an essential function of the organization at a high level and without direct supervision.

Application Procedure

Employer's Responsibilities:

File Form I-129: The US employer submits Form I-129, Petition for a Nonimmigrant Worker, to USCIS with supporting documents showing the qualifying relationship and the employee's executive or managerial role.

Pay Fees: The standard I-129 processing fee and potentially the Fraud Prevention and Detection Fee must be included with the I-129 petition.

Receive Approval: If approved, USCIS sends Form I-797 Notice of Action to the employer, which should be provided to the employee for the visa interview.

Employee's Responsibilities:

Apply for Visa: Upon approval of the I-129 Petition, the employee applies for the L-1A visa at a US embassy or consulate using Form DS-160.

Submit Documents: The employee will need to gather supporting documents, including original Form I-797, passport, photo, and evidence of qualifications, and either submit them with Form DS-160 or present them at the visa interview.

Attend Visa Interview: The employee must attend a visa interview where the consular officer reviews the visa application and will either approve or deny the visa.

Enter the US: If the visa is issued, upon arrival to the US, the employee presents the visa to a CBP officer, is admitted to the US in L-1A status, and receives an I-94 form indicating the period of admission.

Begin Employment: The L-1A employee starts working in the US as an executive or manager.

Blanket L-1A Petitions

Certain organizations that require ongoing personnel transfers may want to streamline the L-1A petition process by filing a blanket petition, establishing the required intracompany relationship in advance.

To qualify for a blanket petition, the following conditions must be met:

Engagement in Commercial Trade or Services: The petitioner and all qualifying organizations must be engaged in commercial trade or services.

US Office Requirements: The petitioner must have a US office that has been doing business for at least one (1) year.

Multiple Branches: The petitioner must have three (3) or more domestic and foreign branches, subsidiaries, or affiliates.

Additional Criteria: The petitioner and the qualifying organizations must meet at least one (1) of the following:

- Have obtained at least ten (10) L-1 approvals in the past twelve (12) months.
- Have US subsidiaries or affiliates with combined annual sales of at least $25 million.
- Have a US workforce of at least 1,000 employees.

Period of Stay

New Office Setup: Employees entering the US to establish a new office are allowed a maximum initial stay of one (1) year.

All Other Employees: Qualified employees entering the US to work at an existing office are allowed a maximum initial stay of three (3) years.

Extensions: Requests for extension of stay may be granted in increments of up to two (2) years, until the employee has reached a maximum limit of seven (7) years.

Family of L-1A Visa Holders

L-1A visa holders may be accompanied or followed by their spouse and any unmarried children under twenty-one (21) years of age. These family members must apply for an L-2 visa. If approved, they are generally granted the same period of stay as the L-1A visa holder. Spouses of L-1A visa holders are eligible to apply for work authorization in the United States under the L-2 visa classification.

13. Intracompany Transferee—Specialized Knowledge: L-1B

What is an L-1B visa?

The L-1B visa is a nonimmigrant visa that allows US employers to transfer employees with specialized knowledge from their foreign offices to their US offices. It also enables foreign companies without a US office to send employees with specialized knowledge to help establish one.

Dual Intention of an L-1B Visa

The L-1B visa is a "dual intent" visa, meaning that the visa holder can legally pursue permanent residency (a green card) in the United States while maintaining their L-1B nonimmigrant status. This is unlike many other nonimmigrant visas that require the holder to prove they do not intend to immigrate permanently to the US.

Dual intent allows L-1B visa holders to start the green card process through employment-based (or other) immigrant visa categories, without the need to leave the US or risk visa denial based on immigrant intent. This dual intent feature makes the L-1B visa particularly attractive for multinational companies and their specialized personnel looking to establish long-term residency in the US.

Eligibility of the US Employer (Petitioner)

To be able to petition for an L-1B employee, the US employer must meet the following criteria:

Qualifying Relationship: The US employer must have a qualifying relationship with the foreign company (parent company, branch, subsidiary, or affiliate).

Business Operations: The US employer must be, or will be, actively doing business in the US and at least one (1) other country, either directly or through a qualifying organization. The business must be regular, systematic, and continuous, and not just the physical presence of an office or agent.

Other considerations:

L-1 Visa Reform Act of 2004

For L-1B petitions involving work at a non-affiliated employer's site, the petitioning employer must demonstrate:

- The employee will not be principally controlled or supervised by the unaffiliated employer.
- The work is not considered labor for hire by the unaffiliated employer.

New Office Setup

For employers seeking to transfer foreign employees to establish a new office in the US, the employer must:

- Secure sufficient physical premises for the new office.
- Demonstrate financial ability to compensate the employee(s) and begin business operations.

Eligibility of L-1B Employee (Beneficiary)

To qualify for an L-1B visa, the foreign employee must meet the following conditions:

Work History: The employee must have worked for a qualifying organization abroad for at least one (1) continuous year within the three (3) years preceding their US admission.

Specialized Knowledge: The employee must possess specialized knowledge relevant to the petitioning employer, including expertise in the company's products, services, research, equipment, techniques, management, or other interests as well as the application of this expertise in international markets.

Application Procedure

Employer's Responsibilities:

File Form I-129: The US employer submits Form I-129, Petition for a Nonimmigrant Worker, to USCIS with supporting documents showing the qualifying relationship and the employee's specialized knowledge and work history.

Pay Fees: The standard I-129 processing fee and potentially the Fraud Prevention and Detection Fee must be included with the I-129 petition.

Receive Approval: If approved, USCIS sends Form I-797 Notice of Action to the employer, which should be provided to the employee for the visa interview.

Employee's Responsibilities:

Apply for Visa: Upon approval of the I-129 Petition, the employee applies for the L-1B visa at a US embassy or consulate using Form DS-160.

Submit Documents: The employee will need to gather supporting documents, including original Form I-797, passport, photo, and evidence of qualifications, and either submit them with Form DS-160 or present them at the visa interview.

Attend Visa Interview: The employee must attend a visa interview where the consular officer reviews the visa application and will either approve or deny the visa.

Enter the US: If the visa is issued, upon arrival to the US, the employee presents the visa to a CBP officer, is admitted to the US in L-1B status, and receives an I-94 form indicating the period of admission.

Begin Employment: The L-1B employee starts working in the US for the petitioning employer.

Blanket L-1B Petitions

Certain organizations that require ongoing personnel transfers may want to streamline the L-1B petition process by filing a blanket petition, establishing the required intracompany relationship in advance.

To qualify for a blanket petition, the following conditions must be met:

Engagement in Commercial Trade or Services: The petitioner and all qualifying organizations must be engaged in commercial trade or services.

US Office Requirements: The petitioner must have a US office that has been doing business for at least one (1) year.

Multiple Branches: The petitioner must have three (3) or more domestic and foreign branches, subsidiaries, or affiliates.

Additional Criteria: The petitioner and the qualifying organizations must meet at least one (1) of the following:

- Have obtained at least ten (10) L-1 approvals in the past twelve (12) months.
- Have US subsidiaries or affiliates with combined annual sales of at least $25 million.
- Have a US workforce of at least 1,000 employees.

Period of Stay

New Office Setup: Employees entering the US to establish a new office are allowed a maximum initial stay of one (1) year.

All Other Employees: Qualified employees entering the US to work at an existing office are allowed a maximum initial stay of three (3) years.

Extensions: Requests for extension of stay may be granted in increments of up to two (2) years, until the employee has reached a maximum limit of five (5) years.

Family of L-1B Visa Holders

Spouses and unmarried children under twenty-one (21) years of age can accompany or follow the L-1B visa holder. These family members must apply for an L-2 visa. If approved, family members are generally granted the same period of stay as the L-1B visa holder, and spouses may apply for work authorization in the US.

14. Specialty Occupation Workers from Australia: E-3

What is an E-3 visa?

The E-3 visa classification is specifically for nationals of Australia who are coming to the United States to perform services in a specialty occupation. A "specialty occupation" requires the application of highly specialized knowledge which typically necessitates the attainment of a bachelor's or higher degree, or its equivalent, in the relevant field as a minimum entry requirement.

Eligibility Criteria

To qualify for an E-3 visa, the applicant must meet the following requirements:

Australian Nationality: The applicant must be a national of Australia.

Employment Offer: The applicant must have a legitimate job offer in the United States.

Qualifications: The applicant must possess the necessary academic or other qualifying credentials for the position.

Specialty Occupation: The job must qualify as a specialty occupation, requiring the theoretical and practical application of specialized knowledge.

Application Procedure from Within the United States

For those applying for an E-3 classification while in the United States, the process involves the US employer filing Form I-129, Petition for Nonimmigrant Worker, on behalf of the Australian worker together with the following supporting documents:

Job Offer Letter: A job offer letter or other documentation from the employer that establishes the applicant will be engaged in a specialty occupation and will be paid either the actual or prevailing wage, whichever is higher.

Labor Condition Application (LCA): An LCA that supports the E-3 classification must be included (for more information on obtaining an LCA, see the section on the H-1B visa).

Academic Credentials: Documentation demonstrating the applicant's qualifications for the specialty occupation.

Licensing: If required, the applicant's license or official permission to practice in the specialty occupation.

Period of Stay

The initial period of stay for an E-3 visa holder is up to two (2) years. Extensions can be granted for up to two (2) years at a time, with no maximum number of extensions, subject to certain exceptions.

Family of E-3 Nonimmigrant Workers

The spouse and unmarried children under twenty-one (21) years of age of an E-3 nonimmigrant worker are entitled to dependent E-3 classification.

Spouses of E-3 workers in valid E-3 or E-3S status are considered employment authorized incident to status, meaning they can work in the United States without needing to apply for separate work authorization. Children of E-3 workers, however, are not permitted to work in the United States.

15. Cultural Exchange Program Visa: Q-1

What is a Q-1 visa?

The Q-1 is a nonimmigrant visa designed for participants in international cultural exchange programs approved by the Department of Homeland Security (DHS). This visa facilitates practical training, employment, and the sharing of the history, culture, and traditions of the participant's home country with the people in the United States.

Special Features of the Q-1 Visa

- **One-Year Outside the US Requirement**: After completing a Q cultural exchange program, participants must spend at least one (1) year outside the US before they may apply for another Q-1 visa. This is to ensure that they do not repeatedly use the Q-1 visa for extended stays in the US. Note that the one (1) year outside the US does not necessarily need to be spent in the applicant's home country or country of last residence.
- **Program Completion**: Participants are expected to leave the US within thirty (30) days of completing their cultural exchange program.

No Dependent Visas: The Q-1 visa does not allow dependents (spouses or children) to accompany or follow the participant to the US.

Eligibility of Participant

Age: At least 18 years old.

Qualifications: Qualified to perform the service, labor, or training.

Cultural Communication: Able to effectively communicate about the cultural attributes of their home country.

Eligibility of Employer

- Only qualified employers or their designated agents (permanently employed in an executive or managerial role) can petition for Q-1 participants.
- The employer must maintain an established international cultural exchange program that includes a cultural element.
- The program must involve practical training and employment while sharing the participant's home country's cultural attributes with the American public.

Petition Process

Form I-129 Submission:

The employer or designated agent must file Form I-129, Petition for a Nonimmigrant Worker, with USCIS together with the required filing fee and supporting evidence (see below).

Supporting Evidence:

- Evidence of the cultural exchange program's design and content (e.g., brochures, curriculum).
- Evidence that the program activities take place in a location where the American public can engage with the foreign culture.
- Evidence that the employer is actively doing business in the US and offering wages and working conditions comparable to local workers.
- Proof of financial capability to compensate the participant (e.g., annual financial report, business tax return).

Visa Issuance: After approval by USCIS, the participant must apply for a Q-1 visa at a US embassy or consulate, if required.

Period of Stay

The initial stay granted to a Q-1 visa holder can be up to fifteen (15) months, depending on the program length. Participants must leave the US within thirty (30) days after completing the program. As mentioned, they must spend one (1) year outside the US before applying for another Q-1 visa.

Family of Q-1 Visa Holders

The Q-1 visa does not allow dependents (spouses or children) to accompany or follow the participant to the US. Family members must qualify independently for Q-1 or other nonimmigrant visas if they want to enter the US.

16. CNMI-Only Transitional Workers: CW-1

What is a CW-1 visa?

CW-1 is a nonimmigrant visa category specifically for temporary workers in the Commonwealth of the Northern Mariana Islands (CNMI). It allows employers in the CNMI to employ foreign workers for a specified period to address labor shortages in various industries.

The CNMI-Only Transitional Worker (CW-1) visa allows employers in the Commonwealth of the Northern Mariana Islands (CNMI) to hire individuals who are not eligible under other nonimmigrant worker categories. This visa program, which is scheduled to end on December 31, 2029, serves as a transitional solution, bridging the gap between the former CNMI foreign worker permit system and the US immigration system.

CW-1 Cap

The CNMI-Only Transitional Worker (CW-1) visa program has an annual cap on the number of visas granted. This cap is applied on a fiscal year basis, running from October 1 to September 30, and covers all workers listed on a single Form I-129CW.

Specific allotments within the cap are set aside for healthcare and certain public utilities occupations and granted on a first-come, first-served basis. Unused visa cap numbers do not carry over to the next fiscal year. However, in the case of a revoked petition, its cap number will be added to the next fiscal year's cap.

The applicable cap is based on the employment start date listed on Form I-129CW. Both new and extension petitions for CW-1 workers are subject to the cap, and USCIS issues alerts when the cap is reached. Petitions submitted after the cap is reached will be rejected unless exempt. Rejected CW-1 extensions will require the foreign worker to leave the CNMI within ten (10) days unless they have obtained another legal status.

Eligibility of Petitioning Employers

To qualify to petition for a CW-1 worker(s), employers must:

- Obtain an approved Temporary Labor Certification (TLC) from the US Department of Labor (DOL) and consider all available US workers for the position.
- Be engaged in a legitimate business, including participation in the E-Verify program (see Chapter 7 for more information on E-Verify).
- Offer employment terms consistent with the nature of their business in the CNMI.
- Comply with federal and CNMI employment requirements, including nondiscrimination, safety, and minimum wage laws.
- Pay reasonable transportation costs if a worker is involuntarily dismissed before their authorized stay ends.
- Comply with semiannual reporting by filing Form I-129CWR, Semiannual Report for CW-1 Employers.

Eligibility of Foreign Workers

To qualify for a CW-1 visa, foreign workers must:

- Be ineligible for other employment-based nonimmigrant visa categories.
- Enter or stay in the CNMI to work in an occupation designated as needing nonimmigrant workers.
- Be the beneficiary of a petition from a legitimate CNMI employer.
- Be lawfully present in the CNMI or otherwise admissible to the US.
- Not be employed in construction or extraction occupations unless they were admitted as a CW-1 during each fiscal year from 2015 through 2018.

CW-1 Application Process

Step 1: Obtain Temporary Labor Certification (TLC)

- The petitioning employer must request a prevailing wage determination (PWD) from the DOL.
- The employer must then use the PWD to apply for a TLC, confirming that no qualified US workers are available and that employing the CW-1 nonimmigrant will not adversely affect US workers.

Step 2: Submit Form I-129CW to USCIS

- The employer must file Form I-129CW with the appropriate fees and approved TLC with USCIS. Note: USCIS will reject petitions submitted without an approved TLC.

Step 3: Apply for Visa

- After Form I-129CW is approved by USCIS, workers outside the US/CNMI will need to apply for a CW-1 visa at a US embassy or consulate.
- Workers already in the CNMI will have their fingerprints and photograph taken at a USCIS Application Support Center if required.

Period of Stay

The initial period of authorized stay is up to one (1) year, which may be extended up to three (3) years in total. After the second renewal, a worker must leave the US/CNMI for thirty (30) days before a new petition may be filed.

The spouse and minor children of a CW-1 worker may apply for CW-2 visas to accompany or join the CW-1 worker in the

CNMI. However, CW-2 dependents' status will expire at the same time as the principal beneficiary's CW-1 status.

If applying from outside the CNMI or requiring consular processing, the CW-1 worker must apply for admission to the US/CNMI within ten (10) days of the petition's validity period to avoid potential revocation of the petition.

Long-Term Worker Exemptions

- Those admitted as a CW-1 during fiscal years 2015 to 2018 may qualify as "long-term workers."
- Long-term workers are exempt from the construction and extraction occupation prohibition and may be granted CW-1 status for up to three (3) years without the temporary departure requirement.

Semiannual Reporting Requirement for CW-1 Employers

Employers with an approved CW-1 petition valid for six (6) months or more must file a Form I-129CWR report to confirm continued employment and compliance with petition terms.

The required timing of the filing of Form I-129CWR is as follows:

Less than six (6) months validity of CW-1: No report required.

Six (6) to twelve (12) months validity of CW-1: File Form I-129CWR six (6) months after the petition start date.

More than twelve (12) months validity of CW-1: File Form I-129CWR every six (6) months up to six (6) months before the petition end date.

Filing Window: Employers must submit Form I-129CWR within sixty (60) days of the six-month anniversary of the petition start date and every six (6) months thereafter.

Documentation: There is no documentary evidence required to be submitted with Form I-129CWR, but the employer should retain employment documents for three (3) years.

Obligations: Employers must report even if the worker is no longer employed with the employer, was never admitted, or has changed status. If the worker is no longer employed by the employer, an explanation should be included.

Additional Note: Employers must also notify USCIS separately if the worker is no longer employed there. Non-compliance may lead to petition revocation or future petition denials.

17. Crewmembers: D

What is a D visa?

The D visa is a nonimmigrant visa for foreign nationals working on commercial sea vessels or international airlines who intend to depart the US within twenty-nine (29) days, either on the same vessel or another vessel. The D visa is specifically designed for individuals working on ships or aircraft, such as deckhands, engineers, and flight attendants, whose primary role is to serve on a vessel or aircraft that operates internationally.

If traveling to the US by other means to join a vessel, a D visa holder must also possess a C-1 (Transit) visa or a combination C-1/D visa to enter the US.

Travel Purposes for Crewmember (D) Visas Include:

- Pilot or flight attendant on a commercial airplane
- Captain, engineer, or deckhand on a sea vessel
- Service staff on a cruise ship
- Trainee on a training vessel

Travel Purposes Not Covered:

- Dry dock repairs: For repairs, a B-1 visa is needed.
- Temporary fishing vessel crew: An H-2 visa is required.
- Coasting officer: For temporary replacement during leave, a B-1 visa is used.
- Private yacht: If on a private yacht that plans to remain in the US for over twenty-nine (29) days, a B-1 visa is necessary.
- Outer Continental Shelf: Requires a B-1 visa.

D Visa Application Process

Submit Online Visa Application: Fill out Form DS-160 and print the confirmation page.

Upload Photo: Upload a photo meeting the specific requirements during the DS-160 process.

Schedule Visa Interview: A personal interview at a US embassy or consulate is required for most applicants aged 14-79; appointment times vary by location.

Attend the Interview: Bring all original supporting documents and pay the visa application fee. If approved, a visa issuance fee may also apply.

Note: As mentioned, for those traveling independently to join a vessel in the US, a C-1 visa is also required. If both visas are requested simultaneously and the conditions for both are met, a combination C-1/D visa may be issued.

Period of Stay

The D visa is typically issued for the length of time needed by the crew member to complete the specific voyage, assignment, or work duties, often up to a few months.

Port of Entry

Crew members holding a D visa can enter the US through any port of entry but must comply with the specific terms of their visa and remain only in the immediate vicinity of the port while not on duty.

Limitations

The D visa does not permit crew members to engage in other employment or stay in the US beyond their authorized period. Additionally, family members of crew members must apply for their own visas in a different visa category (commonly, a B visitor visa) to accompany or join the D crewmember, as the D visa does not provide for dependents.

Departure and Change to Other Visa Category

Crew members on a D visa must depart the US upon completion of their duties. They may be eligible to change their status to another visa category if they meet the requirements, but they must apply for a new visa if they wish to re-enter the US in the future.

18. NAFTA Professionals: TN

What is a TN visa?

The TN nonimmigrant classification is a creation of the North American Free Trade Agreement (NAFTA) which allows Canadian and Mexican citizens of certain professions to seek temporary entry into the US to engage in professional-level business activities. Examples of professions that may meet the eligibility criteria range from accountants, engineers, and scientists to lawyers and teachers. This nonimmigrant status is valid for up to three (3) years and may also be extended.

What are the criteria for a TN visa?

- The applicant must be a citizen of either Canada or Mexico.
- The applicant's profession must qualify under the NAFTA regulation.
- The position in the US must require one of the NAFTA professions.
- The applicant has prearranged either a full-time or part-time job with a specific US employer.
- The applicant has the qualifications and meets the specific requirements, education, or experience required by the profession.

Professions that Qualify Under the NAFTA Regulation

8 CFR 214.6 regulates the types of business activities at a professional level that could qualify citizens of Canada and Mexico to work in the US under TN status.

According to 8 CFR 214.6, "business activities at a professional level" are those undertakings that require an individual to have at least a baccalaureate degree or appropriate credential for successful completion. Appendix 1603.D.1, of this regulation provides a list of professions in which the applicant can show business activity at a professional level. The appendix also gives minimum requirements for qualification for each of the jobs. The complete list of eligible professions can be found at 8 CFR 214.6 NAFTA Regulations.

How to Apply for a TN Visa

The applicant must complete the online nonimmigrant visa application (Form DS-160) and upload a photo in the required format (photo not required if applying in Mexico). Afterward, the applicant will have to schedule an interview at a US embassy or consulate. At the interview, the applicant will be required to pay the corresponding TN visa and reciprocity fees.

Special Arrangements for Canadian Citizens

Canadian citizens are not required to apply for a TN visa at a consulate in Canada. Rather, they may establish eligibility for TN classification at the time they seek admission to the US by providing their documentation directly to US Customs and Border Protection (CBP) at certain CBP-designated US ports of entry or pre-flight inspection stations.

This documentation includes:

- Proof of Canadian citizenship.
- Contract or letter of employment from the US employer providing specific details about the position or professional capacity in which the applicant will work, the purpose of the employment, required educational qualifications, length of stay, evidence of compliance with Department of Homeland Security (DHS) regulations or state laws, and payment arrangements.
- Documentation proving that the applicant meets the minimum education or work experience requirement as stated in CFR 214.6 and Appendix 1603.3.1 of the NAFTA regulation. A credentials evaluation (if the situation demands it) and any applicable fees may also be provided.
- Evidence of applicant's licensure (if required by the job or profession).

Alternatively, if a Canadian citizen has an approved Form-129 petition, he or she may apply for admission to the US as a TN nonimmigrant by merely presenting proof of Canadian citizenship and the Approval Notice of Form I-129 from USCIS.

A list of Designated Ports of Entry where TN applicants can get optimized processing can be found at the following site: https://www.cbp.gov/travel/canadian-and-mexican-citizens/traveling- tn-or-l1-visa-canada.

Usually, there is a $50 charge for getting the TN stamp in the passport at the CBP ports of entry.

Family Members of TN Nonimmigrants

Spouses and unmarried children under the age of twenty-one (21) of TN visa holders may be eligible for TD nonimmigrant status. However, family members are not permitted to work during their stay, and their TD status cannot be extended beyond the period of time granted to the TN nonimmigrant. They are, however, permitted to study during their authorized stay in the US.

For accompanying immediate family members of Canadian TN nonimmigrants, no visa is required. They can enter the US by simply seeking admission at a CBP-designated port of entry and showing:

- Proof of Canadian citizenship
- Proof of relationship (spouse or child) to the TN nonimmigrant.
- Photocopies of the TN nonimmigrant's admission document and proof that that TN nonimmigrant is maintaining their TN status.

Chapter Three:

Employment-Based Immigrant Visas (Green Cards)

———————— ⊠ ————————

As discussed in the previous chapter, there are two categories of employment-based visas: nonimmigrant (NIV) and immigrant (IV). Employment-based NIVs are generally short-term and easier, faster, less expensive, and more readily available to a wider range of workers than immigrant visas.

Employment-based immigrant visas (IVs) also result in the granting of US lawful permanent residence (green cards) to the foreign employee and their immediate family members. However, employment-based IVs tend to have either extremely high standards to meet or lengthy wait times for a visa to become available (or both). On the other hand, unlike NIVs, some employment-based IVs may be obtained without the need for a petition by a US employer (self-petitioning).

The combined processing and wait times for an employment-based immigrant visa may equal several years or even more than a decade—especially if the prospective employee is from a country with an excessive number of applicants, like China or India. Therefore, it is recommended that the employer and prospective employee have a realistic idea of the visa requirements and processing times and craft a plan of action to have the foreign employee on board when needed.

As such, this chapter will detail the requirements for the foreign worker and the type of work or position as well as the responsibilities of both the employer (petitioner) and employee (beneficiary) in the visa application process.

1. First Preference: EB-1

What is an EB-1 visa?

An EB-1 visa is an employment-based immigrant visa (green card) available to foreign nationals who demonstrate extraordinary ability in their field, including sciences, arts, education, business, or athletics. It is also called the "Employment-Based First Preference" category. Spouses and unmarried children under the age of twenty-one (21) of successful applicants may also qualify for green cards.

The EB-1 immigrant visa classification is divided into three (3) separate sub-categories:

1. EB-1A: People with extraordinary abilities
2. EB-1B: Outstanding professors and researchers
3. EB-1C: Multinational managers and executives

EB-1A: Qualifications and Requirements

To qualify for an EB-1A visa, applicants must show that they are among the select few who have risen to the top of their field. One of the main benefits of the EB-1A visa is that it allows for self-petitioning. This means the applicant does not need a company to sponsor them. Instead, the applicant can file a petition on their own behalf.

Securing an EB-1A visa is quite difficult because of the stringent standards, but with proper documentation and legal assistance, it is certainly achievable.

To qualify for an EB-1A visa, there are three (3) main requirements:

1. Applicants must be individuals with extraordinary ability, and they need to provide evidence of their exceptional skills and accomplishments. This can be proved by showing they have received major international awards such as an Oscar, a Pulitzer, an Olympic medal, or a Nobel Peace Prize. However, if they haven't won such an award, they can still qualify if they can provide at least three (3) of the following ten (10) types of evidence as taken from 8 C.F.R. § 204.5(h)(3)(i).

    a. Documentation of the applicant's receipt of lesser nationally or internationally recognized prizes or awards for excellence in the field of endeavor.

    b. Documentation of the applicant's membership in associations in the field for which classification is sought which require outstanding achievements of their members, as judged by recognized national or international experts in their disciplines or fields.

    c. Material of or about the applicant published in professional or major trade publications or other major media relating to the applicant's work in the field for which classification is sought. Such evidence should include the title, date, and author of the material and any necessary translations.

d. Evidence of the applicant's participation, either individually or on a panel, as a judge of the work of others in the same or an allied field of specification for which classification is sought.

e. Evidence of the applicant's original scientific, scholarly, artistic, athletic, or business-related contributions of major significance in the field.

f. Evidence of the applicant's authorship of scholarly articles in the field, professional or major trade publications, or other major media.

g. Evidence of the display of the applicant's work in the field at artistic exhibitions or showcases.

h. Evidence that the applicant has performed in a leading or critical role for organizations or establishments with a distinguished reputation.

i. Evidence that the applicant has commanded a high salary or other significantly high remuneration for services, above others in the field.

j. Evidence of commercial success in the performing arts, as shown by box office receipts or records, cassette, compact disc, or video sales.

2. Applicants must show that they will continue to work in their area of extraordinary ability once they are in the US. This can be proved by showing evidence such as a job offer letter, contracts to work in their field, or other similar evidence.

3. Applicants must also show that their presence in the US will provide a substantial benefit to the country.

Typically, this requirement can be met by showing that they will work in their field of extraordinary ability.

EB-1B: Qualifications and Requirements

The EB-1B sub-category is reserved for professors and researchers who have received international recognition for their outstanding achievements in a particular academic field. To qualify for an EB-1B visa, individuals must show that they are recognized as being outstanding in their academic field. It is worth noting that this standard is somewhat less stringent than the "extraordinary ability" standard required for EB-1A.

Also, unlike EB-1A, EB-1B requires an offer of employment from a prospective US employer. The US employer must also demonstrate that it employs at least three (3) full-time researchers and has documented accomplishments. No labor certification is required, however.

There are three (3) main requirements to qualify for an EB-1B visa:

1. Applicants must show that they are internationally recognized as outstanding in their field. To prove this, they must produce evidence from at least two (2) of the following six (6) categories as listed in 8 C.F.R. § 204.5(h)(3)(i).

    a. Evidence of receipt of major prizes or awards for outstanding achievement.
    b. Evidence of membership in associations that require their members to demonstrate outstanding achievement.

   c. Evidence of published material in professional publications written by others about the applicant's work in the academic field.

   d. Evidence of participation, either on a panel or individually, as a judge of the work of others in the same or an allied academic field.

   e. Evidence of original scientific or scholarly research contributions in the field.

   f. Evidence of authorship of scholarly books or articles (in scholarly journals with international circulation) in the field.

2. Applicants must show that they have three (3) years of experience teaching or conducting research in their respective fields. All three (3) years of experience should be completed before filing the petition for the EB-1B visa.

3. Applicants must also show that they have a job offer in the US to work in a teaching position or as a researcher. There are three (3) types of job offers that will satisfy this requirement:

   a. A job offer as a teacher for a university or institution of higher education,

   b. A job offer as a researcher for a university or institution of higher education, or

   c. A job offer as a researcher for a private employer.

EB-1C: Qualifications and Requirements

The EB-1C visa sub-category is reserved for multinational managers and executives. This visa allows a foreign company to transfer a manager or executive to a related US company. One of the primary benefits of the EB-1C visa is that it does not require the US company to obtain a labor certification through the Department of Labor (DOL). Rather, the US company can directly submit a petition for the foreign worker without undergoing the lengthy process of labor certification first.

To qualify for an EB-1C visa, there are five (5) main requirements:

1. There must exist a qualifying relationship between the foreign company and the US company. There are three (3) types of relationships that satisfy this requirement:

   - Parent/subsidiary.
   - Affiliate; or
   - Branch office.

2. If the applicant is already working for a US-based company, they must have worked for the foreign employer for one (1) year within the three (3) years prior to beginning their work for the US company.

3. The applicant must have worked for the foreign company as a manager or executive.

4. The applicant must have a job offer to work for the US company full-time as a manager or executive.

5. The US company must have been in business for at least one (1) year prior to filing the EB-1C petition.

Procedures and Relevant Documents for Filing EB-1 Petitions

If individuals are applying based on extraordinary abilities (EB-1A), then they do not need to have an employer to file the petition; they can file on their own behalf. The primary document for EB-1A is the I-140 petition. Therefore, the evidence proving the applicant meets the criteria for the EB-1A category must be submitted with the I-140 petition.

For the EB-1B and EB-1C sub-categories, an employer must file the I-140 petition on the foreign national's behalf. Additionally, to demonstrate financial stability, the employer must provide financial statements, audits, and company tax returns.

Processing times for I-140 petitions can vary depending on the visa category. However, as of September 2024, the processing times for the EB-1 classifications were averaging six (6) to eight (8) months. Petitioners have the option to pay an additional fee and request premium processing of the I-140 petition. With premium processing, USCIS adjudicates the petition within fifteen (15) calendar days.

Upon thorough examination of all submitted documents, USCIS will inform all parties of their decision. If the petition is denied, the employer is precluded from recruiting the foreign employee.

If the petition is approved and the beneficiary's priority date is current, they may file an I-485 application to adjust their status to legal permanent resident if they are already in the US. If the beneficiary is abroad or if their priority date is not current, their file will be sent to the National Visa Center (NVC). The applicant will need to complete a DS-260 online immigrant visa application and process their visa at a specified US embassy or consulate.

For more detailed information on both the employment-based adjustment of status and immigrant visa application processes, see Chapter 7.

2. Second Preference: EB-2

What is an EB-2 visa?

An EB-2 visa is an employment-based immigrant visa (green card) available to foreign nationals with advanced degrees or exceptional abilities in the fields of science, arts, or business. Spouses and unmarried children under the age of twenty-one (21) of successful applicants may also qualify for green cards.

The EB-2 immigrant visa classification is divided into three (3) separate sub-categories:

1. **EB-2A (Advanced Degree):** Foreign nationals with a US or foreign equivalent of a master's degree or above or who possess a bachelor's degree plus at least five (5) years of post-baccalaureate experience in the specialized field.
2. **EB-2B (Exceptional Ability):** Foreign nationals who can demonstrate exceptional abilities in the fields of science, arts, or business. They must meet at least three (3) of the following criteria:

- An official academic record showing a degree, diploma, certificate, or similar award from a college, university, school, or other institution of learning related to their area of exceptional ability.

- Letters from current or former employers documenting at least ten (10) years of full-time experience in the field.
- A license to practice the profession or certification for the profession or occupation.
- Evidence of a salary or other remuneration for services that demonstrates exceptional ability.
- Membership in a professional association(s).
- Recognition for achievements and significant contributions to the industry or field from peers, government entities, and professional or business organizations.
- Any other comparable evidence of eligibility.

3. **EB-2C (NIW):** Foreign nationals who meet the requirements of either EB-2A and/or EB-2B <u>and</u> whose work is in the national interest of the United States (see next section, EB-2 with National Interest Waiver).

Application Process

The application process for the EB-2A and EB-2B sub-categories is nearly the same, as both require the petitioning employer to obtain a Program Electronic Review Management (PERM) approval, also known as a "labor certification," from the US Department of Labor (DOL) before filing the immigrant petition. The application process for the EB-2C (NIW) sub-category is completely different and is outlined in detail in the next section (see EB-2 with NIW).

The entire process with the typical timeline for obtaining an EB-2A or EB-2B visa is described below:

1. Apply for Labor Certification (PERM)

Step 1: Formulation of Job Duties and Minimum Requirements

The first step in the labor certification process involves collaboration between the US employer, foreign employee, and preferably, an immigration attorney to establish the crucial details of the job for which sponsorship is being sought. These details include the job title, duties, minimum education and experience requirements, location, scope of supervision, and other vital details.

The employer is responsible for crafting job requirements that align with Department of Labor (DOL) regulations and reflect realistic business needs. Concurrently, the employee must be able to show that they have met the job requirements when accepting the offer, with proper documentation of their relevant previous experience and education. It is important to note that any subsequent changes in the job duties, minimum requirements, or location may necessitate restarting the process.

Step 2: Prevailing Wage Determination

The employer must submit an online Prevailing Wage Determination (PWD) request to the Department of Labor (DOL).

The DOL will determine the prevailing wage for the position in the specified geographic location based on the job duties, minimum requirements, and other details. If the wage for the position is governed by a collective bargaining agreement, the employer is required to submit documentation to the DOL as evidence.

The PWD sets the minimum wage that the employer must be willing to pay the employee when the employee becomes a legal permanent resident. As of July 2024, the DOL is issuing a PWD in a time of four (4) to six (6) months, however, this time may vary.

Step 3: Advertising and Recruitment

In this phase, the employer is required to place a job advertisement in a Sunday newspaper of general circulation for two (2) consecutive Sundays as well as on the State Workforce Agency Website for at least thirty (30) days to attract US workers. This process takes approximately two (2) months. Furthermore, at least three (3) additional types of advertising recruitment measures must be taken and documented.

Advertisements may remain valid for up to one hundred eighty (180) days from the day of the first advertisement. During this period, the employer must follow a strict timeline for these steps and maintain records.

The employer is required to conduct extensive job advertising, interview candidates, and ultimately conclude that no able, willing, qualified, and available US workers can fill the position. If an able, willing, qualified, and available US worker applies for the position, the employer will need to stop the process. The employer must wait at least six (6) months and then re-test the labor market, potentially with a modified criterion.

Step 4: Program Electronic Review Management (PERM) Labor Certification Submission

After the recruitment period concludes without finding any able, willing, qualified, and available US workers, the employer must prepare and file the ETA-9089 PERM application with the DOL, also known as a labor certification (LC) application. However, before moving on to this process, the employer must wait for a cooling-off period of thirty (30) days after the day of the last advertisement. Also, only one (1) of the three (3) aforementioned additional advertising measures may take place within this 30-day period.

As of July 2024, the processing time for a PERM application was about ten (10) to thirteen (13) months, but processing could take significantly longer if the case is audited. However, the chance of the case being audited is small— nationally, the audit rate is about twenty-five (25) percent, but with a comprehensive case preparation (preferably, with legal assistance), the audit rate is less than five (5) percent.

Based on the above, the labor certification (PERM) process can be expected to take approximately sixteen (16) months, or more if there is an audit.

2. Submit Form I-140 (Immigrant Petition)

Once the DOL approves the PERM, the employer must then submit Form I-140, Immigrant Petition for Alien Worker, to USCIS together with the required fees and documentation demonstrating that the foreign employee has the required education, experience, training, and skills for the offered job position. The current USCIS filing fee for Form I-140 is $715.

There is an additional fee that must be submitted with each Form I-140 called the Asylum Program fee, which varies in amount depending on the nature and size of the employer. This fee is currently $600 for employers with more than twenty-five (25) full-time employees and $300 for employers with twenty-five (25) or fewer full-time employees. Non-profit organizations are exempt from this fee.

It usually takes six (6) to nine (9) months to receive a response from USCIS, however, the US employer can opt to pay an additional fee for premium processing and receive an expedited response within fifteen (15) days. If USCIS has any concerns about the petition, they may render a Request for Evidence (RFE), potentially extending the processing time (see Chapter 7 for more information on RFEs).

It is crucial to file Form I-140 within one hundred eighty (180) days of PERM approval as the I-140 must demonstrate the employer's financial capability to pay the wage offered and confirm that the foreign national possesses the education, experience, and skills required in the PERM application. To substantiate financial ability, the employer can submit documents such as profit and loss statements, balance sheets, and even the owner's personal financial information.

3. Wait for Priority Date to Become Current and Apply for Adjustment of Status or an Immigrant Visa

Depending on the visa category and the country of chargeability, an immigrant visa may not immediately be available due to annual quotas on the number of persons allowed to immigrate from each country and in each visa category. However, if the applicant's priority date is current when the PERM is approved, and the applicant is already residing in the US in lawful status, they may be able to file the I-485 (adjustment of status or "green card") application together with the I-140. Otherwise, if the priority date is current at the time of the I-140 approval, then they may be able to file the I-485 application at that time. For detailed information on the employment-based adjustment of status process, see Chapter 7.

If the applicant is residing outside the US and their priority date is current, their approved I-140 petition will be sent to the Department of State's National Visa Center (NVC). The NVC will notify both the petitioning employer and the visa applicant when the petition is received and again when an immigrant visa number is about to become available. At that time, the applicant will need to complete a DS-260 online immigrant visa application and process their visa at a specified US embassy or consulate abroad. Upon issuance of the immigrant visa, the applicant may enter the US and be admitted as a US permanent resident ("green card holder"). For more detailed information on employment-based immigrant visa processing, see Chapter 7.

If, following the approval of the I-140 petition, the applicant's priority date is still not current, the approved petition will be sent to the NVC. The file will remain there until a visa number is available, regardless of whether the applicant is already in the US or not. If the priority date is not expected to become current within three (3) months according to the most recent Visa Bulletin, monitoring services can be utilized to track the progress of visa number availability.

Once the priority date becomes current, if the applicant is in the US in lawful status, they may then choose whether to apply for adjustment of status in the US (Form I-485) or to apply for an immigrant visa at a US embassy or consulate abroad. See Chapter 7 for more detailed information about both of these processes.

3. Second Preference: EB-2 (with NIW)

What is an EB-2 with NIW visa?

An EB-2 with a National Interest Waiver (NIW), also called EB-2C, is an employment-based immigrant visa (green card) where the US government will waive the requirement for a labor certification and employment offer if the foreign national's proposed endeavor is in the country's best interest. As such, this waiver allows the foreign national to self-petition for a visa and avoid the lengthy and uncertain PERM process required of other EB-2 visa applicants (as described in the previous section).

Differences Between a Regular EB-2 Visa and an EB-2 with NIW

While both are employment-based immigrant visa categories, a regular EB-2 and an EB-2 with a National Interest Waiver (NIW) have very different requirements, processing times, and documentation.

Most notably, a regular EB-2 visa requires a formal employment offer and labor certification from the Department of Labor for an applicant to be eligible to apply. In contrast, an EB-2 with NIW does not necessitate an employment offer or labor certification, provided that the foreign national can demonstrate that their admission to the US would be of national benefit. However, all other requirements of an EB-2 visa must still be met to qualify for this visa.

Who qualifies for an EB-2 with National Interest Waiver?

The following individuals are eligible to apply for an EB-2 with NIW:

- A foreign national who meets the educational requirements (see below) or is a person of exceptional ability, and
- A foreign national who meets the three-prong test in the Matter of Dhanasar decision as listed below:

1. The proposed endeavor has substantial merit and national importance;
2. The applicant is well-positioned to advance the proposed endeavor; and
3. On balance, it would be beneficial to the US to waive the requirements of a job offer and labor certification.

Important Things to Know About the NIW

To be eligible for a National Interest Waiver, applicants must fulfill the following:

- **Advanced Degree or Exceptional Ability:** The applicant must either hold an advanced degree (master's degree or higher) or demonstrate exceptional ability in their field. Exceptional ability refers to a level of expertise significantly above that ordinarily encountered in the sciences, arts, or business. In the event the applicant only holds a bachelor's degree or its foreign equivalent, they will be required to demonstrate at least five (5) years of post-baccalaureate progressive work experience in the specialized field.
- **Work in the National Interest:** The applicant's work must be of substantial merit and benefit to the US on a national level. It must be clear that the applicant's contributions are crucial to the country's welfare, and that they will have a more significant impact compared to the work of others in their field. The applicant must show how their proposed endeavor will assist the country in addressing a specific challenge it faces, and that the future goals of the applicant align with similar goals of the US.
- **Waiver of Labor Certification:** Typically, employment-based green card applicants must go through the labor certification process, which involves proving that there are no qualified US workers available for the job being offered to the foreign national. The "on balance" criteria of the NIW refer to the overall assessment of an applicant's qualifications, achievements, and the impact of their work on the US as a whole. When adjudicating an NIW petition, USCIS

considers all the evidence in the aggregate to determine whether, on balance, it supports a finding that the applicant qualifies for the waiver. It is a rigorous standard that requires compelling evidence and a clear demonstration of national benefit.

- **Self-Petition:** The NIW allows applicants to self-petition, meaning they can petition for a green card on their own behalf without requiring a sponsoring employer.

Application Procedure and Requirements

Applying for an NIW allows qualified individuals to bypass the labor certification process typically required for employment-based green card applications, making it an attractive option for those who can demonstrate their work benefits the national interest of the US.

These are the general steps to follow in preparing and submitting a self-petition for an EB-2 with NIW:

1. **Eligibility Evaluation:** The applicant must first determine if they meet the eligibility criteria for an NIW. Generally, they must have an advanced degree (master's or higher) or exceptional abilities in their field, and their work must have a significant impact on the national interests of the US. An individual may also qualify for this type of visa if they have completed a bachelor's degree along with five (5) years of progressive experience.

2. **Category Selection:** There are two (2) categories of NIW applicants: those with advanced degrees and those with exceptional abilities. The applicant needs

to select the appropriate category based on their qualifications, or they can argue both, if applicable.

3. **Form I-140 Petition:** The applicant must complete Form I-140, Immigrant Petition for Alien Worker, as a self-petitioner. This form establishes the applicant's eligibility for an employment-based green card without the need for a labor certification or a specific job offer by demonstrating that their work is in the national interest of the US.

4. **National Interest Statement:** The applicant must include a detailed National Interest Statement explaining how their work benefits or will benefit the US on a national level. The statement should focus on showcasing the significance and impact of the applicant's contributions to their field or industry.

5. **Supporting Evidence:** The applicant should also gather substantial evidence to support the NIW application. This evidence can include publications, awards, citations, letters of recommendation from experts in the field, and any other documentation demonstrating the national importance of the work. Any documents not in the English language should be accompanied by a certified English translation.

6. **Job Offer:** Though an NIW does not require a job offer, having one can strengthen the case. A letter from a current or potential employer stating the applicant's qualifications and how their work benefits the national interest can be included in the application.

7. **Application Submission:** File the completed Form I-140 with the USCIS together with applicable fees and all required NIW supporting documents.

8. **USCIS Decision:** After submission, USCIS will review the immigrant petition and waiver materials. Processing times can vary depending on where the case was filed and the volume of work, so it is essential to be patient. Paying for premium processing can speed up the process of receiving a decision on the waiver, however, it will not affect the remaining waiting time to apply for a green card.

9. **Adjustment of Status or Immigrant Visa:** Depending on the country of chargeability, an immigrant visa may not immediately be available due to annual quotas on the number of persons allowed to immigrate from each country and in each visa category. However, if the applicant's priority date is current when the I-140 is approved and the applicant is already residing in the US in lawful status, they may be able to file the I-485 adjustment of status (green card) application upon approval of the I-140. For detailed information on the employment-based adjustment of status process, see Chapter 7.

10. If the applicant is residing outside the US and their priority date is current, their approved I-140 petition will be sent to the Department of State's National Visa Center (NVC). The applicant will need to complete a DS-260 online immigrant visa application and process their visa at a specified US embassy or consulate abroad. For more detailed information on

employment-based immigrant visa processing, see Chapter 7.

11. If, following the approval of the I-140 petition, the applicant's priority date is still not current, the approved petition will be sent to the NVC. The file will remain there until a visa number is available, regardless of whether the applicant is already in the US or not. If the priority date is not expected to become current within three (3) months according to the most recent Visa Bulletin, monitoring services can be utilized to track the progress of visa number availability.

12. Once the priority date becomes current, if the applicant is in the US in lawful status, they may then choose whether to apply for adjustment of status in the US or an immigrant visa at a US embassy or consulate abroad. See Chapter 7 for detailed information about both of these processes.

A Final Note

It is worth noting that the NIW application process can be complex, and successful applications often require careful preparation and a strong case. Seeking guidance from an experienced immigration attorney can be beneficial to ensure all the requirements are met and increase the chances of a successful outcome.

4. Third Preference: EB-3

What is an EB-3 visa?

An EB-3 is an employment-based immigrant visa (green card) available to foreign nationals who are professional workers, skilled workers, and unskilled workers. It is also called the "Employment-Based Third Preference" category. Within this third preference, a US employer can petition for permanent residence for a foreign employee upon successfully obtaining a PERM approval (labor certification) from the US Department of Labor. Spouses and unmarried children under age twenty-one (21) of successful applicants may also qualify for green cards.

Foreign workers can qualify for an EB-3 visa under three (3) sub-categories:

1. **Professionals:** Individuals whose jobs require at least a US bachelor's degree or its foreign equivalent and who are members of the professions.

2. **Skilled workers:** Individuals who meet the educational, training, or experience requirements of the job opportunity. Relevant post-secondary education may be considered training, and at least two (2) years of job experience is required for this sub-category.

3. **Unskilled workers:** Individuals performing unskilled labor jobs requiring less than two (2) years of training or experience. They do not need to fulfill any educational requirements, and the work does not need to be temporary or seasonal in nature.

EB-3 Application Process

1. Apply for Labor Certification (PERM)

The labor certification process is almost identical for all three (3) EB-3 sub-categories except for the job advertisement step. The entire process, including approximate processing times, is outlined below:

Step 1: Formulation of Job Duties and Minimum Requirements

The first step in the labor certification process involves collaboration between the US employer, foreign employee, and preferably, an immigration attorney to establish the crucial details of the job for which sponsorship is being sought. These details include the job title, duties, minimum education and experience requirements, location, scope of supervision, and other vital details.

The employer is responsible for crafting job requirements that align with Department of Labor (DOL) regulations and reflect realistic business needs. Concurrently, the employee must be able to show that they have met the job requirements when accepting the offer, with proper documentation of their relevant previous experience and education. It is important to note that any subsequent changes in the job duties, minimum requirements, or location may necessitate restarting the process.

Step 2: Prevailing Wage Determination

The employer must submit an online Prevailing Wage Determination (PWD) request to the Department of Labor (DOL).

The DOL will determine the prevailing wage for the position in the specified geographic location based on the job duties, minimum requirements, and other details. If the wage for the position is governed by a collective bargaining agreement, the employer is required to submit documentation to the DOL as evidence.

The PWD sets the minimum wage that the employer must be willing to pay the employee when the employee becomes a legal permanent resident. As of July 2024, the DOL is issuing a PWD in a time of four (4) to six (6) months, however, this time may vary.

Step 3: Advertising and Recruitment

In this phase, the employer is required to place a job advertisement in a Sunday newspaper of general circulation for two (2) consecutive Sundays as well as on the State Workforce Agency Website for at least thirty (30) days to attract US workers. This process takes approximately two (2) months. Furthermore, at least three (3) additional types of advertising recruitment measures must be taken and documented.

Advertisements may remain valid for up to one hundred eighty (180) days from the day of the first advertisement. During this period, the employer must follow a strict timeline for these steps and maintain records.

The employer is required to conduct extensive job advertising, interview candidates, and ultimately conclude that no able, willing, qualified, and available US workers can fill the position. If an able, willing, qualified, and available US worker applies for the position, the employer will need to stop the process. The employer must wait at least six (6) months and then re-test the labor market, potentially with a modified criterion.

Step 4: Program Electronic Review Management (PERM) Labor Certification Submission

After the recruitment period concludes without finding any able, willing, qualified, and available US workers, the employer must prepare and file the ETA-9089 PERM application with the DOL, also known as a labor certification (LC) application. However, before moving on to this process, the employer must wait for a cooling-off period of thirty (30) days after the day of the last advertisement. Only one (1) of the three (3) aforementioned additional advertising measures may take place within this 30-day period.

As of July 2024, the processing time for a PERM application was about ten (10) to thirteen (13) months but could take significantly longer if the case is audited. However, the chance of the case being audited is small—nationally, the audit rate is about twenty-five (25) percent, but with a comprehensive case preparation (preferably, with legal assistance), the audit rate is less than five (5) percent.

Based on the above, the labor certification (PERM) process can be expected to take approximately sixteen (16) months, or more if there is an audit.

2. Submit Form I-140 (Immigrant Petition)

Once the DOL approves the PERM, the employer must then submit Form I-140, Immigrant Petition for Alien Worker, to USCIS together with the required fees and documentation demonstrating that the foreign employee has the required education, experience, training, and skills for the offered job position. The current USCIS filing fee for Form I-140 is $715.

There is an additional fee that must be submitted with each Form I-140 called the Asylum Program fee, which varies in amount depending on the nature and size of the employer. This fee is currently $600 for employers with more than twenty-five (25) full-time employees and $300 for employers with twenty-five (25) or fewer full-time employees. Non-profit organizations are exempt from this fee.

It usually takes six (6) to nine (9) months to receive a response from USCIS, however, the US employer can opt to pay an additional fee for premium processing and receive an expedited response within fifteen (15) days. If USCIS has any concerns about the petition, they may render a Request for Evidence (RFE), potentially extending the processing time (see Chapter 7 for more information on RFEs).

It is crucial to file Form I-140 within one hundred eighty (180) days of PERM approval as the I-140 must demonstrate the employer's financial capability to pay the wage offered and confirm that the foreign national possesses the education, experience, and skills required in the PERM application. To substantiate financial ability, the employer can submit documents such as profit and loss statements, balance sheets, and even the owner's personal financial information.

3. Wait for Priority Date to Become Current and Apply for Adjustment of Status or an Immigrant Visa

Depending on the visa category and the country of chargeability, an immigrant visa may not immediately be available due to annual quotas on the number of persons allowed to immigrate from each country and in each visa category. However, if the applicant's priority date is current when the PERM is approved, and the applicant is already residing in the US in lawful status, they may be able to file the I-485 (adjustment of status or "green card") application together with the I-140. Otherwise, if the priority date is current at the time of the I-140 approval, then they may be able to file the I-485 application at that time. For detailed information on the employment-based adjustment of status process, see Chapter 7.

If the applicant is residing outside the US and their priority date is current, their approved I-140 petition will be sent to the Department of State's National Visa Center (NVC). The NVC will notify both the petitioning employer and the visa applicant when the file has been received. At that time, the applicant will need to complete a DS-260 online immigrant visa application and process their visa at a specified US embassy or consulate abroad. Upon issuance of the immigrant visa, the applicant may enter the US and be admitted as a US permanent resident ("green card holder"). For more detailed information on employment-based immigrant visa processing, see Chapter 7.

If, following the approval of the I-140 petition, the applicant's priority date is still not current, the approved petition will be sent to the NVC. The file will remain there until a visa number is available, regardless of whether the applicant is already in the US or not. If the priority date is not expected to become current within three (3) months according to the most recent Visa Bulletin, monitoring services can be utilized to track the progress of visa number availability.

Once the priority date becomes current, if the applicant is in the US in lawful status, they may then choose whether to apply for adjustment of status in the US (Form I-485) or to apply for an immigrant visa at a US embassy or consulate abroad. See Chapter 7 for more detailed information about both of these processes.

5. Fourth Preference: EB-4

What is an EB-4 visa?

EB-4 is an employment-based immigrant visa category reserved for certain foreign nationals considered "special immigrants." The number of immigrant visas available in the EB-4 category each year is very limited.

Eligibility for an EB-4 Visa

The EB-4 visa was originally intended only for religious workers and other members of non-profit religious denominations who were willing to perform religious duties in the US. However, the EB-4 category has expanded and now covers a wide range of special immigrant classifications through which foreign nationals in a number of different situations can qualify for green cards.

As specifically defined by the Immigration and Nationality Act (INA), those eligible for the EB-4 visa category include:

- Special immigrant religious workers who are ministers or non-ministers within a religious vocation or occupation in a religious organization.
- Special immigrant juveniles (unmarried persons under the age of twenty-one (21)) who live in the US and are dependents of the juvenile court due to abuse, abandonment, or neglect.
- Foreign nationals coming to work in the US as broadcasters for the US Agency for Global Media (USAGM) or a grantee of the USAGM (formerly known as the US Broadcasting Board of Governors).
- Retired G-4 international officers or NATO-6 civilian employees and their families.
- US armed forces members.
- Certain employees of the US government who are currently abroad and their families.
- Foreign nationals who are employees of the Panama Canal Company or Canal Zone government.
- Physicians that were licensed to practice medicine in a US state before January 9, 1978, and were practicing medicine in a state on that date with a J or H visa.
- Certain foreign nationals who have supplied information concerning a criminal organization or enterprise or a terrorist organization, enterprise, or operation (S nonimmigrant visa holders).

Requirements to Obtain an EB-4 Visa

The requirements to apply for an EB-4 visa may vary based on the eligibility group. However, there are a few general requirements listed below:

- The beneficiary (foreign national) needs to have a valid job offer from a financially stable US employer willing to hire them to work in the US. The job cannot be seasonal or part-time. Note: this requirement does not apply to special immigrant juveniles.
- The job offered must be in line with the expertise of the beneficiary.
- The employer must file a petition using Form I-360 along with supplementary documents on behalf of the beneficiary. However, in some specific cases, such as parents, children, and spouses of abusive US citizens, the beneficiary can self-petition. (see Chapter 5, VAWA Self-Petition)
- In the cases requiring a job offer, the beneficiary must have prior experience in the relevant field. For example, special immigrant religious workers seeking to work in the US must have experience working in a religious denomination for a minimum period of two (2) years. Again, this provision does not apply to special immigrant juveniles.

EB-4 Religious Worker Requirements

As mentioned earlier, the most common use of EB-4 immigrant visas is for religious workers. To be eligible, the prospective candidates must fulfill the following mandated qualifications and requirements:

- The applicant must be a member of a religious denomination that has a bona fide non-profit religious organization in the US.
- The applicant must have experience working in said religious denomination for at least two (2) years before the application date.
- The applicant must be seeking admission to the US for the sole purpose of engaging in the vocation of minister in the religious denomination (in the case of ministers).
- The applicant must intend to immigrate permanently, covering a full-time salaried position with the petitioning organization.

As previously mentioned, the number of EB-4 visas available each fiscal year is very limited, and 5,000 of these are allocated for special immigrant religious workers. However, the 5,000 visa cap is not applicable to ministers (there is no cap for ministers).

Application Procedure for EB-4 Religious Workers

Since the number of EB-4 visas allocated for religious workers each year is very limited, interested individuals should start the application process as early as possible, as it may require a considerable amount of time.

The following is an overview of the steps in the application process for an EB-4 visa.

1. **Form I-360 Petition:** The petitioning employer must complete Form I-360, Petition for Special

Immigrant, on behalf of the special immigrant religious worker (applicant).

2. **Religious Worker Letter:** The applicant must obtain a religious worker letter from the superior body of the religious organization operating inside the US. (See below for more information regarding the content of this letter).

3. **Supporting Evidence:** The applicant needs to procure evidence in support of their affiliation with the religious organization and the legitimacy of such an organization to bypass the PERM labor certification requirement. Any documents not in the English language should be accompanied by a certified English translation.

4. **Application Submission:** The employer must submit the completed Form I-360 to USCIS together with applicable fees and all required supporting documents.

5. **USCIS Decision:** After submission, USCIS will review the I-360 immigrant petition and supporting materials. Processing times can vary, depending on where the case was filed and the volume of work. Unfortunately, the option of premium processing is not available for this visa category.

6. **Adjustment of Status or Immigrant Visa:** Upon approval of the I-360, an immigrant visa may not immediately be available due to annual quotas on the number of persons allowed to immigrate from each country and in each visa category. However, if the applicant is residing in the US in lawful status

and their priority date is current, they may be able to file an I-485 adjustment of status (green card) application upon approval of the I-360 petition. This is often the case for individuals in the US on R-1 (religious worker) nonimmigrant visas. In fact, if the priority date is already current at the time of filing the I-360, they may choose to file the I-485 concurrently with the I-360. For more detailed information on the employment-based adjustment of status (I-485) process, see Chapter 7.

If the applicant is residing outside the US and their priority date is current, their approved I-360 petition will be sent to the Department of State's National Visa Center (NVC). The NVC will notify both the petitioning employer and the visa applicant when the file has been received. At that time, the applicant will need to complete a DS-260 online immigrant visa application and process their visa at a specified US embassy or consulate abroad. Upon issuance of the immigrant visa, the applicant may enter the US and be admitted as a US permanent resident ("green card holder"). For more detailed information on employment-based immigrant visa processing, see Chapter 7.

If, following the approval of the I-360 petition, the applicant's priority date is still not current, the approved petition will be sent to the NVC. The file will remain there until a visa number is available, regardless of whether the applicant is already in the US or not. If the priority date is not expected to become current within three (3) months according to the most recent Visa Bulletin, monitoring services can be utilized to track the progress of visa number availability.

Once the priority date becomes current, if the applicant is in the US in lawful status, they may then choose whether to apply for adjustment of status in the US or an immigrant visa at a US embassy or consulate abroad. See Chapter 7 for detailed information about both of these processes.

Content of the EB-4 Religious Worker Letter

The letter for religious workers is a crucial factor in increasing the chances of the EB-4 visa application getting approved, and it must be prepared meticulously with innovative details. Generally, the letter should include information about the applicant's affiliation with the religious organization and the prospects of their position within the organization.

Listed below are some of the details that an EB-4 religious worker letter must contain:

- The letter must demonstrate that the applicant has belonged to the religious organization for at least two (2) years. The letter should also mention that the applicant has at least two (2) years of experience in a religious occupation or vocation.
- For ministers, the letter should contain proof of their authority to minister and details about the duties and responsibilities associated with their occupation.
- For other religious professionals, applicants should have a US bachelor's degree or its foreign equivalent in a field connected to the EB-4 religious worker occupation. The letter should mention this, and the

applicant must also include an official transcript or academic record with the letter.

- In the case of a religious worker, the letter must provide evidence of the applicant's qualifications for the desired religious vocation or occupation.
- In the case of an applicant who intends to work closely with a religious organization in the US but in a non-professional or non-ministerial role, the letter should establish that the US religious organization is affiliated with the applicant's religious denomination.
- Finally, the applicant's letter must explain in detail the duties of the minister or the expected wages to be received by the professional or worker. The letter should testify that the applicant will not rely on charitable organizations or side sources of income for financial sustenance.

Advantages of Applying for a Visa in the EB-4 Category

1. PERM labor certification is not required if the applicant has authentic proof of their affiliation with a religious organization operating in the US.
2. There is also the possibility for adjustment of status from nonimmigrant to immigrant, saving the applicant the time and expense of leaving the US and consular processing. This is often the case for individuals already in the US on R-1 (religious worker) nonimmigrant visas.
3. The process is relatively speedy compared to other visa categories.

4. As with all immigrant visa categories, the applicant can apply for dependent immigrant visas for their spouse and any unmarried children under twenty-one (21) years of age.

Disadvantages of Applying for a Visa in the EB-4 Category

1. The major drawback of the EB-4 visa category is that it is subject to a very low annual cap (cap-subject). Only 10,000 immigrant visas are allocated each year under this category, of which 5,000 are reserved for special immigrant religious workers (except for the minister position, which is not cap-subject).

2. There is no premium processing available for this visa category, which means one cannot expedite the petition processing time. Rather, applicants must wait several months for USCIS to respond within its usual processing time.

3. Applicants from countries with a high volume of immigrant visa applicants (such as China or India) might have a longer waiting period for their priority date to become current.

6. Adjustment of Status (Form I-485): Employment-Based Cases

Overview

The I-485 application is a vital last step in obtaining lawful permanent residency (a green card) in the US.

This section is intended specifically for foreign workers who have an approved or pending I-140 petition (employment-based immigration), are residing in the US in lawful status, and are eligible to adjust their status to that of a US lawful permanent resident. However, the required documents and steps to the I-485 application process outlined below are similar for beneficiaries of family-based, investor, humanitarian, and other immigrant visa categories.

Basics of the Employment-Based I-485 Application Process

The employment-based I-485 application allows eligible individuals to complete the process of applying for a green card within the US without the necessity to depart the country and apply for an immigrant visa at a US embassy or consulate abroad (consular process). To be eligible, the applicant must have an approved or receipted I-140 petition and meet all other requirements for adjustment of status. In cases where a visa number is immediately available, applicants can file the I-140 and I-485 concurrently.

Eligibility Requirements for the Employment-Based I-485 Application

To proceed with the employment-based I-485 application, the following requirements must be met:

1. **Approved or Receipted I-140 Petition:** The applicant must have an approved or receipted Form I-140, Immigrant Petition for Alien Worker, confirming that the applicant meets the eligibility criteria for an employment-based immigrant visa.

2. **Priority Date Current:** The priority date, as indicated on Form I-797 Notice of Action (receipt notice) for the I-140 petition, must be current according to the Visa Bulletin issued by the US Department of State. Note: A "priority date" is typically the date the USCIS received the immigrant petition. A "current" priority date means visa numbers are available for individuals with the applicant's priority date, country of origin, and visa category.

3. **Lawful Status:** The applicant must have continuously maintained lawful nonimmigrant status in the US from the most recent entry until the filing of the I-485 application.

4. **Eligibility Category:** The applicant must fit into one of the eligible employment-based categories as specified in the visa bulletin.

5. **Admissibility:** The applicant must be admissible to the US, meaning they must not have any disqualifying factors such as criminal history, health-related issues, or security concerns.

Documents for the Employment-Based I-485 Application

An employment-based I-485 application requires a comprehensive set of supporting documents from the primary applicant and all accompanying family members in the US.

This list includes, but is not limited to:

- **Form I-485:** Completed and signed Form I-485, Application to Register Permanent Residence or Adjust Status.
- **Identity Documents:** Clear and legible copies of each applicant's passport, birth certificate, and other identification documents (with English translations, if applicable).
- **Form I-797:** Copy of the Form I-797 Notice of Action confirming the approval or receipt of the I-140 petition.
- **Passport Photos:** Two passport-sized photos of each applicant, adhering to the specifications outlined by the US Citizenship and Immigration Services (USCIS).
- **I-94 Arrival/Departure Record:** A copy of each applicant's most recent I-94 arrival/departure record.
- **Medical Examination:** Medical examination for each applicant conducted by a USCIS-approved civil surgeon. The sealed exam results, documented on Form I-693, must be included with the application.
- **Marriage and Birth Certificates:** Birth and marriage certificates (with English translations, if applicable) for accompanying family members only.
- **Employment Letters:** Letter(s) from current and/or previous employers confirming the primary applicant's work history, job duties, and other relevant employment details.
- **Evidence of J-1/J-2 Home Residency Requirement Compliance:** In the case of an applicant who currently holds or previously held J-1/J-2 status, evidence of compliance with the two-year home

residency requirement or an approved waiver of this requirement.

- **Form G-28:** A completed Form G-28, Notice of Entry of Appearance as Attorney, if represented by an attorney.

Additionally, an I-485 application may be accompanied by the filing of additional USCIS forms such as Form I-131 application for advance parole (travel permit while the case is pending), Form I-765 application for employment authorization (work permit while the case is pending), Form I-601 (waiver of inadmissibility), and Form I-864 (affidavit of support), if required.

Fees

The current I-485 fee is $1,440 for each adult and $950 for each child under fourteen (14) years of age. Additional forms such as I-131 and I-765 each have a corresponding fee. Fees may be paid by check or money order. They may also be paid by credit or debit card using Form G-1450, Authorization for Credit Card Transactions.

Biometrics Appointment

Typically, one (1) to two (2) months after the submission of the required I-485 paperwork, the applicant and all accompanying family members over age fourteen (14) will receive a notice to appear for a biometrics appointment. This appointment will be scheduled at the nearest Application Support Center (ASC) to the applicant's place of residence.

During the biometrics appointment, each applicant will provide their fingerprints, photograph, and signature. This information is used to conduct a background check and to create an identification document as part of the immigration process. It's important to attend the scheduled biometrics appointment or to reschedule it in advance, if necessary, as failing to do so can cause delays in the I-485 application processing or even lead to a denial of the application.

Applicants should bring the biometrics appointment notice, a valid government-issued photo ID (such as a passport or driver's license), and any other documents requested in the appointment notice to the appointment. It's also recommended to arrive at least fifteen (15) minutes early to allow for check-in procedures.

I-485 Interview with USCIS Officer

The time between the filing of Form I-485 and when the applicant receives the personal interview notice can vary significantly. This timeline depends on several factors, including the specific USCIS office handling the case, the current workload of that office, and the specifics of the case itself. The processing times can be quite lengthy, often taking several months to over one (1) year.

At the I-485 interview, an immigration officer will review the applicant's green card application and the documentation and information supporting the green card application. Specifically, in the case of an employment-based I-485 application, the applicant will need to confirm that the job offer is still available for them and produce all the original civil documents (birth certificates, marriage certificates, etc.), immigration status documents (H-1B approvals, visa stamps, SEVIS documents, etc.), as well as the sealed medical exam results (if not previously submitted with the I-485 application).

After the interview, green cards are typically approved and mailed to the applicants within a range of two (2) weeks to two (2) months, although this timeline can vary. On rare occasions, when Visa Bulletin retrogression occurs and a visa number is no longer available after a successful interview, the I-485 file will be sent to the National Benefits Center. In that scenario, the USCIS will place the application on hold and will approve and issue a green card as soon as a visa number becomes available again.

Conclusion

The I-485 application is a significant final step to obtaining permanent residency in the US. By understanding the basics of the process, meeting all requirements, and providing complete, accurate, and timely documentation, applicants and their family members in the US can navigate this crucial step successfully.

7. Immigration Visa Processing (IVP): Employment-Based Cases

Overview

Immigrant visa processing (IVP), also known as "consular processing" is a vital last step in obtaining US lawful permanent residency (a green card) for beneficiaries who are either residing outside the US or who are in the US but not eligible to apply for adjustment of status. This process involves beneficiaries applying for an immigrant visa at a US embassy or consulate in their home country or, in some cases, a third country and then being admitted to the US as permanent residents (green card holders).

This section is intended primarily for foreign workers (and their accompanying family members) who:

Have an approved I-140 petition (employment-based immigrant petition); and

Are residing outside the US; or

3) Are in the US but are not eligible to apply for adjustment of status.

As detailed in Chapters 2 and 3, there are various employment-based immigrant visa categories, including but not limited to:

- EB-1: Priority Workers (for individuals with extraordinary ability, outstanding professors/ researchers, and multinational executives/managers)
- EB-2: Professionals with Advanced Degrees or Exceptional Ability
- EB-3: Skilled Workers, Professionals, and Other Workers
- EB-4: Special Immigrant Visas (for religious workers, certain international employees, etc.)
- EB-5: Immigrant Investors

Each category has specific criteria and requirements to qualify, which are outlined in Chapters 2 and 3.

Eligibility Requirements for IVP

To initiate Immigrant Visa Processing for an employment-based application, the following general requirements must be met:

- Approved I-140 Petition: The applicant must have an approved Form I-140, Immigrant Petition for Alien Worker, confirming that the applicant meets the eligibility criteria for an employment-based immigrant visa.
- Job Offer: In some cases, the applicant has to provide a valid and approved job offer from a US employer.
- Employment Visa Category: The applicant must qualify under one (1) of the employment-based visa categories mentioned above (EB-1, EB-2, EB-3, EB-4, EB-5), depending on their qualifications and eligibility.
- Current Priority Date: Employment-based visas often have a limited number of annual slots, and a "priority date" will be established based on the date of the petition's filing. When the applicant's priority date becomes current, a visa number becomes available, and they may begin immigrant visa processing.

Required Documents for the IV Application

An employment-based immigrant visa application requires a comprehensive set of supporting documents from the primary applicant and all accompanying family members.

This list includes, but is not limited to:

- Form DS-260, Immigrant Visa Electronic Application: The primary applicant and each accompanying family member must complete this form online through the Consular Electronic Application Center (CEAC) and submit it electronically.
- I-140 Approval Notice: Copy of Form I-797 Notice of Action confirming the approval of the I-140 petition.
- Birth Certificate: Copy of each applicant's birth certificate, which indicates the proper birth date, parents' names, and birthplace.
- Online Birth Registration: This document is solely applicable to Bangladeshi applicants.
- Marriage Certificate: To verify the marital relationship, an accompanying spouse is required to submit this document. Muslim applicants must also provide a copy of their *Nikahnama*.
- Divorce Certificate: Required of all applicants (if applicable).
- Passport: All applicants must submit the biographic pages of their current passport.
- Police Certificate: Required from all countries where any applicant over age sixteen (16) has resided for more than six (6) months or where they may have an arrest record.
- NVC Welcome Notice Copy: Each applicant must submit a copy of the complete NVC Welcome Notice and the checklist.
- Occupational Field Confirmation Letter (self-petitioners only): A duly signed statement is required to confirm the applicant's unequivocal intention to

pursue employment in the specific occupational field as indicated in Form I-140. This requirement applies solely to the primary applicant.

- Any other documents requested by the NVC and/or USCIS.

Consular Appointment/Interview

In the case of consular processing, once a visa is available or the priority date is current (earlier than the cut-off date listed in the monthly Visa Bulletin), the consular office will notify the petitioner and beneficiary (applicant) and schedule the applicant and any accompanying family members for an in-person appointment/interview. They will also notify the applicant(s) when they must submit the immigrant visa processing fees (also known as "fee bills") and the required supporting documentation.

On the day of the interview, the applicant(s) should bring the originals of all the required documents. During the interview, the consular officer will review the application information and documents and decide if the applicants are eligible for an immigrant visa.

Visa Approval and Entry to US

Upon approval of the immigrant visas, the consular officer will give a packet of information to each applicant. This packet is known as a "Visa Packet" and must not be opened. A USCIS Immigrant Fee, which USCIS will use to process the immigrant visa packet and produce the physical green cards, must be paid at this moment.

After arriving in the United States, the applicant(s) will need to give the Visa Packet to the US Customs and Border Protection (CBP) officer at the port of entry. The CBP officer will inspect each applicant and determine whether to admit them into the United States as a lawful permanent resident. If the CBP officer admits the individual(s), they will then have lawful permanent resident status and be able to live and work in the United States permanently. The individuals will receive the physical "green cards" in the mail several weeks later at the US address they provided.

Conclusion

Immigrant visa processing is a significant final step to obtaining permanent residency in the US. By understanding the basics of the process, meeting all requirements, and providing complete, accurate, and timely documentation, applicants and their family members can navigate this crucial step successfully.

Chapter Four:

Application Process Articles

—————————— ▱ ——————————

T his chapter includes a number of articles specifically intended for HR professionals—namely those responsible for reviewing, documenting, and tracking new hire employment authorization credentials—to clarify and assist with this process and ensure the company is always in DHS compliance.

Each section provides an overview of the required steps, forms, and supporting documents for each process. However, as always, more specific and updated information regarding current policies, fees, filing locations, and processing times may be found on the USCIS website (www.uscis.gov) or by consulting with a qualified US immigration attorney or legal service.

1. Verifying Employment Authorization Documents (EADs)

Overview

In the United States, employers must verify that all employees, regardless of citizenship or national origin, are legally authorized to work in the US. For foreign nationals who are not US permanent residents (green card holders), especially those who were <u>not</u> sponsored for employment by the company, this often involves presenting an Employment Authorization Document (EAD), officially known as Form I-766.

Types of Employment Authorization Documents (EADs)

The US Citizenship and Immigration Services (USCIS) issues three (3) main types of EADs:

Initial EAD: Validates that an individual is authorized to work in the US for the first time.

Renewal EAD: Extends the validity of an initial EAD. Renewal applications are generally filed no more than one hundred and eighty (180) days before the original EAD expires.

Replacement EAD: Replaces a lost, stolen, or damaged EAD or one issued with incorrect information.

Visa Categories Eligible for an EAD

Verifying an employee's EAD involves understanding which categories of nonimmigrant visas and other immigration benefits can qualify for an EAD.

1. **Nonimmigrant Visa Categories**:
   o **F-1 Students**: Eligible for Optional Practical Training (OPT) or Curricular Practical Training (CPT), including a 24-month STEM extension for qualifying students.

- o **J-1 Exchange Visitors**: Eligible for work authorization related to their exchange program. J-2 dependents may also apply for an EAD.
- o **M-1 Students**: Can apply for Practical Training related to their field of study.
- o **H-4 Dependents**: May qualify for an EAD if the spouse has an approved I-140 immigrant petition or meets specific conditions.
- o **L-2 Dependents**: Eligible to apply for an EAD.
- o **B-1 Business Visitors:** May occasionally receive EADs under specific conditions.

2. **Asylum Seekers and Refugees**:
- o **Asylees**: Eligible for an EAD while their asylum application is pending or approved.
- o **Refugees**: Can apply for an EAD for work authorization while adjusting to permanent residency.

3. **Employment-Based Visa Categories**:
- o **E-1/E-2 Treaty Traders/Investors**: E-1 and E-2 visa holders, including their dependents, may apply for an EAD if granted specific employment authorization.
- o **Visa Holders**: Recognized for extraordinary ability or achievement, O-1 visa holders may apply for an EAD under certain conditions.
- o **TN Visa Holders**: Professionals from Canada and Mexico on TN visas under NAFTA may be eligible for an EAD if certain criteria are met.

4. **Victims of Crime or Trafficking**:
   - **U Visa Holders**: Victims of certain crimes holding a U visa can apply for an EAD.
   - **T Visa Holders**: Individuals trafficked into the US who hold a T visa status may apply for an EAD.
3. **Special Categories and Programs**:
   - **Deferred Action for Childhood Arrivals (DACA)**: Individuals granted DACA status may apply for an EAD as part of their deferred action status.
   - **Temporary Protected Status (TPS)**: Nationals from designated countries with TPS are eligible for an EAD while their status is valid.
   - **VAWA Self-Petitioners**: Individuals self-petitioning under the Violence Against Women Act (VAWA) may qualify for an EAD while their petition is pending.

How to Verify Eligibility

On the front center of the EAD, there is the word "Category" with a three-digit code under it. The code is comprised of a letter and two (2) numbers that reference the visa category or other immigration benefit program through which the EAD was authorized. Knowing the program through which the employee obtained the EAD can help HR professionals to verify if the cardholder is authorized to engage in employment in the particular position or company.

The following is a comprehensive list of EAD category codes:

- **(a)(2)**: Lawful Temporary Resident
- **(a)(3)**: Refugee
- **(a)(4)**: Paroled refugee

- **(a)(5)**: Asylee
- **(a)(6)**: Fiancé(e) (K-1 or K-2 nonimmigrant)
- **(a)(7)**: N-8 or N-9
- **(a)(8)**: Citizen of Micronesia, Marshall Islands, or Palau
- **(a)(9)**: K-3 or K-4
- **(a)(10)**: Withholding of Deportation or Removal granted
- **(a)(11)**: Deferred Enforced Departure
- **(a)(12)**: Temporary Protected Status granted
- **(a)(13)**: Family Unity Program (Section 301 of the Immigration Act of 1990)
- **(a)(14)**: LIFE Legalization (Section 1504 of the Legal Immigrant Family Equity (LIFE) Act Amendments)
- **(a)(15)**: V nonimmigrant
- **(a)(16)**: T-1 nonimmigrant
- **(a)(17)**: Spouse of an E nonimmigrant
- **(a)(18)**: Spouse of an L nonimmigrant
- **(a)(19)**: U-1 nonimmigrant
- **(a)(20)**: U-2, U-3, U-4, or U-5 nonimmigrant
- **(c)(1)**: Spouse/dependent of A-1 or A-2 nonimmigrant
- **(c)(2)**: Spouse/dependent of Coordination Council for North American Affairs (E-1)/ Taipei Economic and Cultural Representative Office (TECRO)
- **(c)(3)(A)**: F-1 student, pre-completion Optional Practical Training
- **(c)(3)(B)**: F-1 student, post-completion Optional Practical Training
- **(c)(3)(C)**: F-1 student, 24-month extension for STEM students

- **(c)(3)(ii)**: F-1 student, off-campus employment sponsored by a qualifying international organization
- **(c)(3)(iii)**: F-1 student, off-campus employment due to severe economic hardship
- **(c)(4)**: Spouse/dependent of G-1, G-3, or G-4
- **(c)(5)**: J-2 spouse or child of J-1 exchange visitor
- **(c)(6)**: M-1 student, Practical Training
- **(c)(7)**: Dependent of NATO-1 through NATO-6
- **(c)(8)**: Asylum application pending filed on/after January 4, 1995
- **(c)(8)**: Asylum application pending filed before January 4, 1995, and applicant is not in exclusion/deportation proceedings
- **(c)(8)**: Asylum application pending filed before January 4, 1995, and applicant is in exclusion/deportation proceedings
- **(c)(8)**: Asylum application under ABC Agreement
- **(c)(9)**: Pending adjustment of status under Section 245 of the Act
- **(c)(10)**: Suspension of Deportation applicants (filed before April 1, 1997), Cancellation of Removal applicants, and Cancellation applicants under NACARA
- **(c)(11)**: Public Interest parolee
- **(c)(12)**: Spouse of an E-2 CNMI investor
- **(c)(14)**: Deferred Action
- **(c)(15)**: Not in use
- **(c)(16)**: Creation of Record (adjustment based on continuous residence since January 1, 1972)

- **(c)(17)(i)**: B-1 domestic servant of certain nonimmigrants
- **(c)(17)(ii)**: B-1 domestic servant of certain US citizens who are in the United States on a temporary basis
- **(c)(17)(iii)**: Certain B-1 nonimmigrant employees of a foreign airline
- **(c)(18)**: Order of Supervision
- **(c)(19)**: Certain pending TPS applicants whom USCIS has determined are prima facie eligible for TPS and who may then receive an EAD as a "temporary treatment benefit" under 8 C.F.R. 244.10(a)
- **(c)(20)**: Section 210 legalization (pending I-700)
- **(c)(21)**: S nonimmigrant
- **(c)(22)**: Section 245A legalization (pending I-687)
- **(c)(23)**: Irish Peace Process (Q-2)
- **(c)(24)**: LIFE legalization
- **(c)(25)**: T-2, T-3, T-4, T-5, or T-6 nonimmigrant
- **(c)(26)**: Spouse of an H-1B nonimmigrant
- **(c)(27)**: Abused spouse of an A nonimmigrant
- **(c)(28)**: Abused spouse of an E-3 nonimmigrant
- **(c)(29)**: Abused spouse of a G nonimmigrant
- **(c)(30)**: Abused spouse of an H nonimmigrant
- **(c)(31)**: VAWA self-petitioners with an approved Form I-360
- **(c)(33)**: Consideration of Deferred Action for Childhood Arrivals (DACA)
- **(c)(35)**: Principal beneficiary of an approved employment-based immigrant petition facing compelling circumstances

- **(c)(36)**: Spouse or unmarried child of a principal beneficiary of an approved employment-based immigrant petition facing compelling circumstances

EADs and Implications for Employers

It is important to understand that EADs (work permits) are not the same as green cards or visas and that they are quite temporary in nature—commonly issued for periods of only one (1) year at a time. Therefore, it is essential for HR professionals to have a system in place to track the expiration dates of EADs and follow up with employees in a timely manner to update their documents/I-9s accordingly.

Also, EADs themselves are not immigration status. They are temporary permits issued to individuals who either a) have a pending immigration case, b) are the derivative family members of a nonimmigrant visa holder, or c) are the beneficiaries of a temporary benefit program so they may support themselves financially while their case is pending or while they or a family member is in the US temporarily. While some EAD holders may be on a path to US permanent residence, others may only have a temporary or nonimmigrant status in the US.

Therefore, if an employer is interested in keeping an employee with an EAD on staff long-term or permanently, it is helpful to know the basis for which the EAD was issued as well as other available immigration pathways (as outlined in this book) to determine if an employment-based petition for that employee may be something to consider.

2. Verifying Employee Identity and Authorization for US Employment (Form I-9)

Overview

US employers must verify that all employees, regardless of citizenship or national origin, are legally authorized to work in the US. To accomplish this, each employee and employer must complete Form I-9. Using this form, the employee must attest to their immigration/citizenship status and present valid evidence of their eligibility to work in the US, and the employer must verify and document this evidence.

How and When to Complete Form I-9

Form I-9 has two (2) sections and two (2) supplements. Section 1 must be completed by the employees themselves (through the use of a translator, if needed) by the end of their first day of employment with the company. In this section, the employee provides basic personal information and attests to their nationality/authorization to work in the US. If the employee has the assistance of a translator or preparer to complete Section 1, then Supplement A must be completed and signed by the translator or preparer.

Section 2 must be completed by the employer (usually an HR professional) or an authorized representative of the employer within three (3) days of the employee's start date. In Section 2, the documents presented by the employee demonstrating their eligibility to work in the US are examined for authenticity and noted. In the case of a rehire or an employee whose documents need to be reverified, then Supplement B must be used.

Section Two contains three (3) lists of acceptable documents that an employee may present. The employee, regardless of which box they check in Section 1, has the option to present either one (1) document from List A (which demonstrates their identity plus their eligibility to work in the US) or one (1) document from List B (identity) and one (1) document from List C (eligibility to work in US). The employer may *not* designate specifically which documents the employee must present.

List A: Documents That Establish Both Identity and Employment Authorization (All documents must be unexpired):

- US passport or US passport card
- Form I-551, Permanent Resident Card (Green Card)
- Foreign passport with a temporary I-551 stamp or notation
- Form I-766, Employment Authorization Document (EAD) with a photograph
- Passport from the Federated States of Micronesia (FSM) or the Republic of the Marshall Islands with Form I-94

List B: Documents That Establish Identity (All documents must be unexpired):

- Driver's license or ID card issued by a US state or possession
- ID card from federal, state, or local government agencies

- School ID card with a photograph
- Voter's registration card
- US military card or draft record
- Native American tribal document

For individuals under age eighteen (18) who cannot present any of the documents listed above, acceptable alternatives include:

- School record or report card
- Clinic, doctor, or hospital record
- Daycare or nursery school record

List C: Documents That Establish Employment Authorization (All documents must be unexpired):

- US Social Security Account Number card (without restrictive notations)
- Certification of report of birth issued by the US Department of State
- US birth certificate with an official seal
- Native American tribal document
- Form I-197, US Citizen Identification Card
- Employment authorization issued by DHS (e.g., Form I-94 Arrival/Departure Record (this would be used by H-1B employees and other work-authorized nonimmigrants), Form I-571 Refugee Travel Document, Form I-327 Reentry Permit, etc.) Note: These are *not* the same as Form I-766 Employment Authorization Document (EAD) mentioned in the List A documents.

Acceptable Receipts

Employees may present receipts for certain documents temporarily. Acceptable receipts include:

- Receipt for a replacement of a lost, stolen, or damaged List A document
- Form I-94 issued to a lawful permanent resident with an I-551 stamp
- Receipt for a replacement of a lost, stolen, or damaged List B or List C document

Verifying Document Authenticity

HR professionals completing I-9 forms have the responsibility to examine the documents for authenticity to the best of their ability and verify the identity and employment eligibility of each employee. Nevertheless, with increasing improvements in technology and document falsification, this can be a difficult task for a non-expert.

Here are some tips for employers and their HR staff to ensure that the employees they hire are authorized to work in the US and that the company is always DHS-compliant.

Using E-Verify: Employers may use E-Verify to electronically confirm the employee's work eligibility in the US. (See the following section on E-Verify for more details)

Consulting with a false documents expert: Some immigration attorneys and other legal or law enforcement experts may be willing to provide a training session to HR staff on how to identify false green cards, work permits, social security cards, and other documents typically presented for the I-9.

Being familiar with the basics of EADs (work permits): Ensure the document is valid, not expired, and correctly reflects the employee's eligibility category. (See next section for more details on EAD types and categories)

Tracking document expiration dates: Maintain accurate records and monitor expiration dates of EADs and other temporary work authorizations (e.g. H-1B, R-1, O-2, etc.)

3. E-Verify

Overview

E-Verify is an online system that enables employers to confirm the employment eligibility of their employees in the United States. Established under the Illegal Immigration Reform and Immigrant Responsibility Act of 1996 (IIRIRA), this web-based program allows employers to verify that employees are legally authorized to work by comparing information from the employee's Form I-9 with records from the US Department of Homeland Security (DHS) and the Social Security Administration (SSA). The system provides results within seconds, confirming whether an employee's details match the government records.

Why Use E-Verify?

The primary purpose of E-Verify is to ensure compliance with US immigration laws, specifically the Immigration Reform and Control Act (IRCA) of 1986, which mandates that employers verify the identity and work eligibility of their employees. By using E-Verify, employers can confirm that their workforce consists of individuals legally authorized to work in the US, thereby mitigating the risk of legal issues related to unauthorized employment.

The E-Verify Process

1. **Enrollment:**
   - **Visit the Enrollment Website:** Begin by visiting the E-Verify enrollment website and agreeing to the terms. (www.e-verify.gov)
   - **Set Up Account:** Create an Enrollment Point of Contact (POC) account and select the access method.
   - **Provide Company Information:** Provide basic details about the company, including legal name, address, and Employer Identification Number (EIN).
   - **Complete Hiring Site Information:** Indicate the number of hiring sites and their participation status in E-Verify.
   - **Sign MOU:** Review and agree to the Memorandum of Understanding (MOU) and submit the enrollment.

2. **Verification:**
   - **Create a Case:** Use information from the employee's Form I-9 to create a case in E-Verify.
   - **Get Results:** E-Verify compares the details with DHS and SSA records and provides an initial result within seconds.
   - **Resolve Mismatches:** If there is a mismatch, notify the employee and allow them to resolve the issue.

○ **Finalize Case:** Close the case once a final result is received, which may include Employment Authorized, Tentative Nonconfirmation, or Final Nonconfirmation.

Benefits of E-Verify

1. **Enhanced Compliance:**
   ○ E-Verify ensures adherence to federal immigration laws, helping avoid fines and penalties related to unauthorized employment.

2. **Streamlined Hiring:**
   ○ Automates the verification process, reducing the time and effort needed to complete paperwork and onboard new employees efficiently.

3. **Fraud Reduction:**
   ○ Minimizes the risk of hiring individuals with fraudulent documents, thereby protecting the company from potential legal issues.

4. **Workplace Safety:**
   ○ Enhances security by confirming that only authorized individuals are employed, which helps in maintaining restricted areas within the business.

5. **Stronger Audit Defense:**
   ○ Demonstrates good faith in compliance practices, which is beneficial in the event of an immigration audit.

6. **Support for Visa Applications:**
   ○ Provides supporting documentation for visa applications, showing a commitment to legal employment practices.

7. **Government Benefits:**
   - o Potential eligibility for government contracts, grants, or incentives in certain states.
8. **HR Integration:**
   - o Seamlessly integrates with existing HR systems for efficient management of employee data and compliance tracking.
9. **Cost Savings:**
   - o Saves time and resources by improving the hiring process and reducing fraud, which can lead to increased productivity and profitability.

4. Visa vs. Status

Overview

The term "visa" is often used loosely to describe any type of immigration benefit; however, a visa is a specific, physical document that not all individuals in the US legally necessarily possess. More often than not, when talking about a person's "visa" what is really meant is the individual's "status" in the US, that is to say, the specific visa category or other type of immigration benefit for which they have been permitted to enter or remain in the US. Both terms and how they relate to each other will be explained in detail below.

What is a Visa?

A visa is a stamp or sticker placed in a passport that serves as an entry document for individuals seeking admission into the United States. Whether the intent is a short-term visit (e.g., a tourist) or a longer stay (e.g., an H-1B worker), obtaining a visa from a US embassy or consulate outside the United States is necessary to enter the country. However, the visa itself only grants the right to *request* entry; the decision whether to admit the individual is made by the immigration officer at the port of entry. Once admitted, the visa becomes less significant, and the focus shifts to the individual's *status*.

What is Status?

Status refers to the legal condition under which an individual is admitted to the US and includes a set of rights and responsibilities depending on the category (e.g., F-1, J-2, H-1B, E-2, etc.), each with distinct regulations and benefits. Upon arrival at a port of entry, in addition to a visa, the individual must show the necessary documents, such as an I-20 for students or an H-1B approval notice for workers, to demonstrate eligibility for admission in that category. If the documentation is compliant, the immigration officer places an entry stamp in the passport, indicating the immigration status category and its expiration date. In cases like F-1 or J-1 students, the status may be listed as "D/S" (Duration of Status), which ties the end date of status to the I-20's expiration. Adherence to the regulations of status is crucial, as violations can lead to the loss of status and other serious consequences.

Key Difference between Visa Expiration vs. Status Expiration

A visa is solely an entry document and can expire while the individual remains in the US without impacting their legal status. As long as the status is valid and the regulations are followed, the person can stay legally in the US until the authorized end date of their status, even if the visa itself expires. However, a valid visa is necessary for re-entry into the US after international travel. If the visa has expired, obtaining a new one is required before re-entering the US.

Visa Validity and International Travel

The validity period of a visa is determined by reciprocity agreements between the US and the applicant's home country, leading to varying lengths of validity as well as number of entries allowed. However, as mentioned, the visa's expiration date does not affect the end date of the individual's status. Once admitted, the visa's validity is no longer a factor until the individual departs and seeks re-entry. Even if the visa expires while the individual is still in the US in lawful status, there is no immediate need for renewal unless the individual plans to travel internationally.

The Role of Status in Determining Length of Stay

The length of stay in the US is established by the inspecting officer assigning status duration upon entry. Some statuses have a fixed end date, while others offer flexibility, such as "Duration of Status" (D/S) for F and J statuses. D/S allows individuals to remain in the US as long as they maintain their status, with additional grace periods for program completion. For F status, this includes a 60-day grace period; for J status, a 30-day grace period.

Status Changes and Visa Requirements

Status changes can occur without impacting the need for a new visa. For example, individuals on Optional Practical

Training (OPT) or those transferring their SEVIS record to a new school may continue their authorized stay in the US without the need for a new visa. Individuals in many different nonimmigrant visa categories often apply for an extension of their current status or a change to a different status, both of which can be processed from within the US without the necessity to obtain a new visa. Likewise, an individual may opt to renew or change their status by obtaining a new visa abroad and re-entering, depending on their needs and circumstances.

Renewing a Visa

Renewing a visa is necessary only when: a) planning to re-enter the US after international travel and b) the current visa has expired or the individual plans to re-enter the US in a different visa category. Applying for a new visa must be done at a US embassy or consulate, typically in the individual's home country, although in a third country is also possible. The process mirrors the initial visa application process in terms of demonstrating eligibility for the particular visa category.

5. Change/Extension of Status Application (Form I-539)

Overview

If an individual with valid nonimmigrant status wants to either change to a different nonimmigrant status or extend their current status while remaining in the United States, they can file a request with US Citizenship and Immigration

Services (USCIS) before their authorized stay expires. This procedure is known as a change/extension of status, for which Form I-539 or I-539A must be filed.

Exceptions

- It is not necessary to apply for a change of nonimmigrant status to attend school in the US if one is the accompanying spouse or child of an individual in A, E, G, H, I, J, or L status. In addition, dependents of F and M visa holders may attend elementary, middle, or high school, but if they want to attend post-secondary school full-time, then they must apply for a change of status.
- Form I-539 cannot be used to request an extension of stay in or change of status to the following visa categories: E-1, E-2, E-3, H-1B, H-1B1, H-2A, H-2B, H-3, L-1, O-1, O-2, P-1, P-2, P-3, P-1S, P-2S, P-3S, Q-1, R-1, TN-1, and TN-2.
- Applying for a change of nonimmigrant status is not allowed if admitted to the US with a C, D, K, or S nonimmigrant visa or through the Visa Waiver Program unless the individual wants to change to T or U nonimmigrant status.
- A vocational student (M-1) may not apply for a change of status to F-1, H-1B, H-1B1, H-2A, H-2B, or H-3.
- An international exchange visitor (J-1) generally may not change nonimmigrant status if admitted to the United States to receive graduate medical training or if their program has a foreign residence requirement unless a waiver is requested and granted. If a waiver is

not granted, only an application to change to an A or G visa status is allowed.

Eligibility Requirements

A foreign national must obtain permission from USCIS to extend their current status or change to another nonimmigrant status before lawfully continuing or beginning to engage in new activities.

An individual may apply to extend or change status in the US if:

- Lawfully admitted into the US as a nonimmigrant.
- No act has been committed that would make them ineligible to receive an immigration benefit.
- There is no factor requiring them to depart the United States and re-enter in order to extend or change nonimmigrant classification (for example, in some cases a new visa must be obtained prior to being readmitted into the United States).
- Form I-539 application for an extension or change of status is submitted by mail or online before the expiration date shown on the admission stamp in the travel document or on Form I-94, Arrival/Departure Record. (There are certain very limited circumstances under which USCIS will excuse a late submission.)

Required Forms

- Form I-539 (or I-539A for co-applicants)
- Form I-907 (only applicable for individuals requesting a change of status to F-1, F-2, M-1, M-2, J-1, or J-2).

Required Documents

- Most recent Form I-94
- Documents proving identification (passport, visa, driver's license, etc.)
- Documents proving maintenance of current lawful status
- Documents proving familial relationship to the primary visa holder (for dependents only)
- Documents proving lawful status of primary visa holder (for dependents only)
- Documents proving financial ability (for F-1 and M-1)
- Form I-20 (for F-1 and M-1)
- DS-2019 (for J-1)
- Form I-566 (for A and G visa dependents)
- Written statement

Timeline

Typically, processing takes two (2) to six (6) months, with some cases receiving a decision sooner. Applicants requesting a change of status to E-1 dependent, E-2 dependent, E-2C, E-3, F-1, F-2, H-4, M-1, M-2, J-1, J-2, L-2, O-3, P-4, or R-2 nonimmigrant status can request premium processing (for an additional fee) and receive a decision within thirty (30) business days once all the prerequisites, including receipt of biometrics results, have been met.

6. Request for Evidence (RFE)

Overview

An RFE is a notification sent by USCIS to an applicant or petitioner for an immigration benefit indicating that the officer reviewing the case requires more information before they can make a decision.

An RFE does *not* mean that the application/petition is going to be denied or even that it is more likely to be denied. An RFE is more like a second chance to review an application/petition and ensure that the applicant/petitioner has provided the most compelling evidence, that all statements mentioned in the package filed are real, and that the applicant, petitioner, or beneficiary is indeed eligible for the requested benefit.

Why an RFE Is Created and What It Includes

The USCIS Policy Manual provides clear guidelines on how to review each type of petition or application filed. In addition to outlining general eligibility requirements, the manual has charts and checklists that officers can use while reviewing applications. These guidance materials define the situations where issuing an RFE is appropriate.

As such, there are RFE templates that give USCIS officers a starting point. Officers can then customize these templates to request more information and/or documents for individual applications/petitions. The key parts of an RFE generally include the facts, the law, the evidence already submitted, the evidence lacking, and the deadline to respond.

What to Do After Receiving an RFE

After receiving an RFE, the applicant/petitioner (and their attorney, if any) should read the entire notice carefully. It is very important to understand each part of the RFE. After reading the full RFE, the applicant/petitioner should review the original application/petition package and prepare an RFE response to submit to USCIS.

Tips for Preparing an RFE Response

Typically, an RFE will only be issued once, giving the applicant a single opportunity to address all remaining questions USCIS has about the application/petition. Therefore, comprehending every detail in the notice and responding accurately is essential.

Generally, an RFE specifies a deadline for response, which cannot be extended. This deadline is the most crucial part of the RFE response and will be stated either as a date or as a number of days. If it is given as a number of days, count the days from the date on the first page of the RFE (the date the RFE was issued), not from the date the RFE was received. Failure to submit the response on time could result in the denial of the application or petition due to late submission or non-submission.

Another important aspect to note is that the original RFE notice, which contains a unique number, must be submitted with the response materials. Therefore, it is mandatory to keep the original notice safe and place it on top of the response package materials before mailing.

Since there is only a single original RFE notice, it is essential to submit all requested evidence in the same package. Partial submission of documents may lead USCIS to consider the response as a request for a decision based on the existing record. Generally, only single copies of each requested document should be submitted, however, duplicate copies may be needed when requesting consular notification.

All documents submitted in the RFE response package must be in English. If a document is in another language, it must be accompanied by a complete English translation. The translator must certify that the translation is accurate and that they are competent to translate from that language to English.

USCIS typically indicates what information is missing by specifying which documents have been submitted and which are still required. They also provide guidance as to the types of documents that will satisfy the requested evidence. It is crucial to submit as much relevant documentation as possible. If any requested document cannot be provided, an explanation is required along with alternative evidence, if possible.

Lastly, paying attention to the address for RFE submission is crucial, as it is usually different from the address where the original application or petition was filed. The RFE notice specifies the response submission address, and the entire response must be sent to that address in a single package.

Prior to sealing the response package, it is advisable to photocopy all of the response materials, including the original RFE notice. When mailing the response package to

USCIS, it is advised to use a tracking service that includes confirmation of delivery. Keeping proof of delivery together with the photocopied RFE package materials will help maintain a complete record of the submission.

7. Notice of Intent to Deny (NOID)

Overview

A Notice of Intent to Deny (NOID) is a formal notification from USCIS indicating that an immigration petition or application is at risk of denial. This notice is issued when the reviewing officer identifies significant concerns such as insufficient evidence, discrepancies, or other issues that could affect the outcome of the application. The NOID serves as a final opportunity to address these concerns before a final decision is made.

Meaning of "Intent to Deny"

The term "Intent to Deny" reflects USCIS's preliminary determination that the application, as it stands, does not meet the required criteria for approval. However, it is important to note that a NOID is not an outright denial but rather a warning that action is needed to resolve the identified issues.

Common Reasons for Issuing a NOID

Several factors may lead to the issuance of a NOID, including:

- **Insufficient Evidence:** The initial submission may lack adequate supporting documentation.

- **Failure to Meet Eligibility Criteria:** The applicant may not meet the specific requirements for the visa or benefit sought.
- **Discrepancies or Errors:** There may be mistakes or inconsistencies in the application or supporting documents.
- **Violation of Immigration Laws:** Violations or false information may have come to light during the review process.
- **Inadmissibility:** There may be criminal convictions or circumstances that render the applicant inadmissible to the US.

NOIDs can also be issued due to new evidence or information that contradicts previous findings, such as a criminal conviction or a violation of US immigration laws.

Impact of a NOID on a Green Card (I-485) Application

For those applying for permanent residence (a green card), a NOID indicates that USCIS has significant concerns about the I-485 application. These concerns must be addressed promptly to avoid denial. The NOID will outline the specific reasons for the potential denial, providing a roadmap for addressing the issues and strengthening the case.

Difference Between NOID and Request for Evidence (RFE)

While both a NOID and a Request for Evidence (RFE) are issued to seek additional information, they serve different purposes:

- **Request for Evidence (RFE):** Issued when specific documents or information are missing, incomplete, or insufficient. An RFE asks for additional evidence to complete the application.
- **Notice of Intent to Deny (NOID):** Issued when USCIS identifies more serious issues that could lead to denial. A NOID requires a comprehensive response to address significant concerns or deficiencies.

A NOID typically reflects a more serious concern than an RFE and indicates that the application is at greater risk of denial unless the issues are resolved.

Steps to Take After Receiving a NOID

While receiving a NOID should prompt immediate action, as the notice is time-sensitive, it is essential to remain calm and methodical in preparing a response.

The following steps are recommended:

1. **Gather Additional Evidence:** Collect all relevant documents, evidence, or information requested in the NOID. Consider any additional evidence that might strengthen the case. An "over-evidencing" approach is advisable to address all concerns raised by USCIS.
2. **Update Existing Documents:** Review and update any documents flagged as problematic by USCIS. For instance, if applying for an E-2 investor visa, a business plan may require revisions in budgeting and forecasting. Ensure that these changes are clearly referenced in the covering letter.
3. **Include a Cover Letter:** A well-organized cover letter is essential for providing clarification on the

content of the new documents and any revisions made. This letter should guide the reviewing officer through the response, highlighting how the new evidence addresses the concerns raised.

4. **Consult Legal Expertise:** Given the complexity of immigration law and the specific requirements for responding to a NOID, it is advisable to consult an experienced immigration attorney. An attorney can help in crafting a compelling response and ensuring that all procedural and evidentiary requirements are met.

NOID Response Deadline and Processing Time

A response to a NOID must be submitted within the timeframe specified by USCIS, typically thirty (30) to thirty-three (33) days from the date of issuance. Missing this deadline can result in the application being denied without further consideration.

Once USCIS receives the response, the review process can take several months or even longer, depending on the complexity of the case and the evidence provided. During this time, it may be necessary to apply for an extension of the current visa status to maintain lawful status.

Denial Following a NOID

If the petition or application is denied after responding to a NOID, several options may still be available, depending on the type of visa or benefit sought:

- **File a Legal Motion:** It may be possible to file a motion to reopen or reconsider the decision.

- **Explore Other Immigration Options:** Consider other immigration pathways that may be available.
- **Consult an Attorney:** Legal guidance can be crucial in understanding the best course of action and navigating the appeal process.

Chapter Five:

Federal Litigation

---◻︎---

U nfortunately, not all petitions and applications for immigration benefits will be approved or even processed within a reasonable time. Some cases simply do not meet the requirements for the benefits sought, and others may not have been prepared or filed correctly or supported with sufficient documentation. This is why it is highly recommended that employers who wish to hire foreign workers first consult with an immigration law professional, especially for more complex cases.

Fortunately, there are several legal alternatives that an applicant can turn to in the event they receive an unfavorable decision or have been waiting an excessively long time for a response or decision on their case, causing undue harm.

The chapter outlines two legal processes (writ of mandamus and administrative appeal) that are available to foreign nationals and their petitioning employers whose cases have been either excessively delayed or incorrectly denied. While the applicant may or may not have had legal help in preparing their original case, it is highly recommended that they seek a qualified immigration law attorney if interested in pursuing one of these federal litigation alternatives.

1. Writ of Mandamus

What is a Writ of Mandamus?

A writ of mandamus is a civil action lawsuit that seeks to compel a government entity to take action on a specific matter or case. A mandamus lawsuit will not necessarily result in the approval of a case, but it does imply that the government or agency must act in accordance with the law's requirements. A mandamus lawsuit can be filed for certain nonimmigrant and immigrant visa cases that have been unreasonably delayed as well as adjustment of status and naturalization (citizenship) applications that are taking well beyond the usual processing time to adjudicate. The applicant must first establish that they have exercised all available administrative remedies before filing a petition for a writ of mandamus.

A writ of mandamus is not the same as an appeal. In a mandamus lawsuit, a higher court only orders a lower court to make a ruling on a specific issue, but it does not instruct the agency on how to rule. In an appeal, the higher court would be asked to rule that the lower court made a mistake in deciding the case.

When can a writ of mandamus be filed?

Although there is no specified time limit to file a mandamus petition, a petition may be dismissed if considered to have been filed too late.

Statutory Framework of Writ of Mandamus

Some of the types of applications that could be eligible for mandamus are U visas, EADs, H-1B visas, F-1 visas, I-485s (including I-485s based on Diversity Lottery visas), and naturalization applications. Applicants who have been harmed due to the unreasonable delay in the processing of their applications can opt for a writ of mandamus.

The following are the relevant statutory provisions that deal with mandamus lawsuits, as found in the Mandamus and Administrative Procedure Act (APA):

28 USC. § 1361: The District Court shall have original jurisdiction of any action in the nature of mandamus to compel an officer or employee of the United States or any agency thereof to perform their duty owed to the Plaintiff.

5 USC. § 555(b): The agency shall proceed to conclude a matter before it within a reasonable time, considering the convenience and necessity of the parties or their representatives.

5 USC. § 706: To the extent necessary to decision and when presented, the reviewing court shall decide all relevant questions of law, interpret constitutional and statutory provisions, and determine the meaning or applicability of the terms of an agency action. The reviewing court shall compel agency action unlawfully withheld or unreasonably delayed.

Writ of Mandamus Elements

To succeed in a mandamus petition, these three (3) elements must be established:

1. The plaintiff has a clear right to the requested relief,

2. The agency has a clear duty to perform the act at issue, and

3. There are no other available adequate remedies.

1. The plaintiff has a clear right to the requested relief: The relief being requested is not an order to grant the benefit but rather an order for the corresponding agency to decide on the application. The Administrative Procedures Act (APA) clearly states that if a decision has been delayed for an unreasonable amount of time, the applicant can file a lawsuit called the "Writ of Mandamus" in the federal courts of the United States. In the lawsuit, a federal judge can be asked to order the Executive Branch (including USCIS and the Department of State) to decide or adjudicate the case within a few months.

2. The agency has a clear duty to perform the act at issue: If a person has the right to apply for a benefit, then the agency also has a duty to act on the application. This duty to act is also reflected in regulations that require the agencies to "issue" a decision. In this case, the government has an affirmative duty to issue or make a final decision within a "reasonable" time.

3. There are no other available adequate remedies: Mandamus lawsuit addresses issues that are not covered by other legal remedies. This also means that, when no other adequate legal remedy is available and the petitioner has exhausted all possible administrative remedies, they are eligible for a writ of mandamus.

Outcomes of Writ of Mandamus

Filing a writ of mandamus frequently serves as a stern nudge to the corresponding agency (in this case, the Department of Homeland Security or DHS) to act on the case. Once a mandamus lawsuit has been filed, DHS may decide to adjudicate the application or avoid the case entirely. If DHS decides on the application before the deadline to respond to the lawsuit, then the matter is closed.

In other cases, DHS will choose to pursue the writ of mandamus in court. DHS has sixty (60) days to reply to the lawsuit by submitting either an answer or a petition to dismiss. If DHS finds that the applicant is not eligible for the immigration benefit or there are sufficient grounds to reject the application, then the application may be rejected based on those grounds. But if the court finds that unreasonable delay has occurred on the part of the government agency (DHS), it will order DHS to timely adjudicate or decide on the case and issue a final decision.

A writ of mandamus compels government agencies to issue a timely final decision on a case. Ideally, this action could result in a fast approval for the applicant. However, as much as there is a possibility of getting a faster approval, there is also a chance of receiving a faster denial. In either case, a writ of mandamus can provide peace of mind by ending a long and indefinite waiting period.

185

Writ of Mandamus Limitations

There are certain limitations to a mandamus lawsuit:

1. The Mandamus Act does not provide a separate, substantial basis for a lawsuit.
2. The court cannot compel an agency to exercise its discretion in any particular manner in a case before it.
3. The court cannot compel the agency to grant a case or provide a remedy in the Plaintiff's favor.

2. Administrative Appeals

What is an Administrative Appeal?

An administrative appeal is a written request to a higher authority to review an unfavorable decision. In the case of a petition or application to the US Citizenship and Immigration Services (USCIS) that is denied, the decision can be appealed to the Administrative Appeals Office (AAO). Administrative appeals end in one of four (4) possible outcomes: the initial judgment may be reversed, dismissed, modified, or left unchanged.

Types of Immigration Appeals

There are a variety of appellate processes for decisions on US immigration petitions and applications. The avenue to follow is determined by (a) the type of petition or application submitted, (b) whether the individual has valid immigration status, and (c) whether the individual is detained in an immigration detention facility.

There are six (6) main types of immigration appeal processes:

1. Appeals before the AAO
2. Appeals before the BIA
3. Criminal alien appeals
4. Habeas corpus, Mandamus, and APA actions
5. Petitions for Review to the US Court of Appeals
6. Motions to reconsider/motions to reopen

What types of immigration issues can be brought before the Administrative Appeals Office?

The Administrative Appeals Office (AAO) exclusively examines decisions made by officers of the US Citizenship and Immigration Services (USCIS).

The AAO can hear appeals of approximately fifty (50) different types of immigration applications and petitions, including:

1. Most employment-based immigrant and nonimmigrant visa petitions (Forms I-140 and I-129)
2. EB-5 immigrant investor petitions (Form I-526) and Regional Center applications (Form I-924)
3. Temporary Protected Status applications (Form I-821)
4. K-1 Fiancé(e) visa petitions (Form I-129F)
5. Applications for a waiver of inadmissibility (Form I-601)
6. Applications for permission to reapply for admission after removal/deportation (Form I-212)

7. Certain special immigrant visa petitions (Form I-360) except for Form I-360 widower appeals, which are appealable to the BIA

8. Orphan petitions (Forms I-600/I-600A and I-800/I-800A)

9. T and U visa applications and petitions (Forms I-914 and I-918) and the related adjustment of status applications (Form I-485)

10. Applications for certificates of citizenship (Form N-600) and applications to replace certificates of naturalization and citizenship (Form N-565)

11. Applications to preserve residence for naturalization purposes (Form N-470)

12. Determinations by Immigration and Customs Enforcement (ICE) of a surety bond breach

How to File an AAO Appeal

When USCIS denies a petition or application, the agency sends the petitioner or applicant a letter detailing why the petition or application was denied. The letter will include instructions on filing an appeal or a motion for reconsideration if the decision can be challenged. Most appeals must be filed using USCIS Form I-290B.

I-290B Notice of Appeal or Motion

Use this form to file:

1. An appeal with the Administrative Appeals Office (AAO);

2. A motion for reconsideration with the USCIS office that issued the latest decision in a case (including a field office, service center, or the AAO); or

3. An appeal of a denial of Form I-17, Petition for Approval of School for Attendance by Nonimmigrant Student, by the Immigration and Customs Enforcement (ICE) Student and Exchange Visitor Program (SEVP).

This form should NOT be used to file:

1. An appeal by the <u>beneficiary</u> of a petition. Generally, only the applicant or petitioner may file an appeal or motion. Exception: The beneficiary of Form I-140, Immigrant Petition for Alien Worker, may use Form I-290B to file an appeal only if USCIS revoked the approved Form I-140 and advised the beneficiary that they may file a motion or appeal. The USCIS revocation notice must be included with Form I-290B.

2. An appeal with the Board of Immigration Appeals (BIA). Note: Appeals of Form I-130, Petition for Alien Relative, fall under the appellate jurisdiction of the BIA. The BIA also has jurisdiction over appeals of self-petitions by widow(er)s using Form I-360, Petition for Amerasian, Widow(er), or Special Immigrant. In these cases, the petitioner must file an appeal with the BIA using Form EOIR-29, Notice of Appeal to the Board of Immigration Appeals.

3. An appeal of a USCIS "no risk" determination under the Adam Walsh Act. In this case, the applicant may seek "further review" by filing a motion to reopen or

reconsider using Form I-290B. However, there is no true appeal option available for such a determination.

4. An appeal of a Department of State consular officer's denial of a US visa application (Forms DS-156, DS-156E, DS-156K, DS-117, DS-157, DS-230, or DS-260). Note: There is no appeal option for a denied Form DS-160. More information can be found on the Department of State website regarding denials of US consular visa applications.

5. An appeal of a Special Agricultural Worker or Legalization application. These appeals must be filed using Form I-694, Notice of Appeal of Decision, under Sections 245(a) and 210 of the Immigration and Nationality Act.

How to Submit Form I-290B

Appellants should refer to the Direct Filing Addresses for Form I-290B, Notice of Appeal or Motion page on the uscis.gov website to send their appeal or motion for reconsideration to the correct address. Form I-290B should not be mailed directly to the AAO.

Part Two:
Helpful Information about Immigration Forms

Chapter One:

Investment-Based Immigration

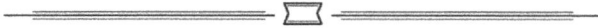

———————— ⬭ ————————

This chapter outlines several types of visas and other programs designed for foreign nationals and their employees who wish to enter the US for the purpose of either starting, investing in, or doing trade with a new or existing US business. The purpose behind these programs is to create more job opportunities for US workers and foster the growth of the US economy.

These may not be the categories of visas that an HR professional would commonly encounter—unless they are working at a company funded by foreign investors. However, employers should be aware of these and all immigration avenues available to current or prospective employees in the event an individual may qualify for a different benefit that is better suited to their or the company's needs and goals.

1. Treaty Traders: E-1

What is an E-1 visa?

An E-1 visa, also known as the Treaty Traders visa, is a nonimmigrant visa category that enables a national of a treaty country to enter the US for the sole purpose of carrying out substantial trade between the US and their home country.

Here, "trade" denotes the international exchange of goods, and a "treaty country" is one a) with whom the US maintains a treaty of commerce and navigation, b) with whom the US maintains a qualifying international agreement, or c) that has been deemed a qualifying country by legislation. A list of the eligible treaty countries is provided and regularly updated by the US Department of State.

Certain employees of a qualified E-1 trader (individual or organization) may also be eligible for this visa. However, a US employer cannot petition for E-1 status for an employee, as this visa classification is specifically set aside for foreign nationals, including foreign employers, with an existing treaty.

What are the requirements to get an E-1 visa?

- The applicant must be a citizen of a country that has a relevant treaty with the US (as described above).
- The trading firm in the US on whose behalf the applicant plans to come to the US must have the treaty country's nationality, meaning that at least fifty (50) percent of the enterprise must be owned by persons with the treaty country's nationality. Additionally, more than fifty (50) percent of the international trade involved must be between the US and the treaty country.
- The international trade must be "substantial," meaning a sizable and continuing trade volume exists.

- If the applicant is an employee of an E-1 trader, then they must be an "essential" employee, meaning they are employed in a supervisory or executive capacity, or they possess highly specialized skills essential to the efficient operation of the firm. Nonessential skilled or unskilled workers do not qualify.
- The applicant must provide evidence that they plan to depart the US following the termination of their E-1 visa status.

Additionally, if the E-1 trader is a business (rather than an individual), at least fifty (50) percent of the business must be owned by treaty country nationals.

In the case of E-1 employees, normally only employees who are nationals of that treaty country are eligible for an E-1 employee visa; however, there is one exception to this rule:

According to 9 FAM 402.9-4(B) Nationality and 9 FAM 402.9-5(D), if the business is owned equally by nationals of two (2) treaty countries, it can be considered a joint venture. In this situation, nationals of either of these two (2) countries are eligible for an E-1 visa.

Required Documents for E-1 Visa

Applying for an E-1 can be done either from within the US through USCIS or from outside the US through a US consulate or embassy. Regardless of the method chosen, the required documents are as follows:

- Valid passport
- Evidence that the applicant meets the conditions to be eligible for E-1 status

- Information about the foreign company in the US, such as what type of business they conduct, what their scope of business is, and who owns the business. They should also include documentation such as evidence of substantial trade, articles of incorporation, certificates of ownership, financial statements, and copies of business plans
- Evidence that the applicant intends to leave the US following termination of E-1 status, such as a foreign property deed and/or a signed statement detailing plans to reside in a foreign country upon termination of E-1 visa status

In addition to the above-mentioned documents, E-1 employees will require a letter from the employer detailing their position in the company and stating that they possess highly specialized skills essential for the efficient operation of the firm or that they hold an executive or managerial position.

Applying for E-1 Status/Visa

1. Applying from within the US

Those who are already legally residing in the US can change their status by filing Form I-129, Petition for a Nonimmigrant Worker, with the United States Citizenship and Immigration Services (USCIS). The applicant must submit evidence of their ownership, nationality, substantial trade, and proof of previous status. In the case of an E-1 employee of the E-1 trader, evidence must be submitted to prove that the employee will principally and primarily perform executive or supervisory duties or that they possess special qualifications essential to the enterprise. For more information about Change/Extension of Nonimmigrant Status, See Chapter 7.

If the E-1 applicant is residing in the US without legal status, they will have to depart the US and apply for a visa at a US embassy or consulate abroad (see below).

2. Applying from outside the US

If the applicant is outside the US, they will have to apply for an E-1 visa at a US consulate or embassy abroad. The applicant first needs to complete and submit Form DS-160 online. While completing Form DS-160, the applicant will also upload a visa photo as per the format explained in the Photograph Requirements. In addition, all E-1 treaty trader visa applicants need to submit a nonimmigrant Treaty Trader/Treaty Investor Application, Form DS-156E. After filing the forms, the applicant will be given a confirmation page and code which will be needed for the consular interview.

At the appropriate time, the candidate will schedule a personal interview with a consular officer. The estimated wait time for visa interviews can be checked through the website of the respective US embassy or consulate. During the interview, the applicant may be asked various questions about the E-1 business, their personal background, and their immigration plans. After successfully completing the interview, the applicant should have the E-1 visa stamped into their passport within a few days. With the E-1 visa stamp, the applicant will be able to enter the US based on the terms of the visa and, upon entry, receive an I-94 with E-1 status.

Although the overall time to process an E-1 visa abroad varies depending on many factors, such as the time of year and the individual consulate, a general estimate on a timeline can be somewhere between two (2) to four (4) weeks from the filing of the application.

Note: The specific steps and processing times for nonimmigrant visas can vary from country to country as well as change over time. It is important to always refer to the website of the specific embassy or consulate where the processing will be done for the most updated information.

Length of Stay in US

The maximum period for an E-1 visa to be issued is two (2) years, however, there is no limit on the number of extensions that can be issued to E-1 visa holders.

E-1 visa status can be extended in two (2) ways. One way is to travel outside the US and then re-enter. This way, there will be an automatic renewal for another two (2) years and a new I-94 will be provided.

The other way is by filing Form I-539, Application to Extend or Change Status. If the individual remains qualified for E-1 status, a two-year extension will be granted. E-1 visa holders can also extend their stay in the US by applying to change status if they become qualified for another category of visa. For more information about Change/Extension of Nonimmigrant Status, See Chapter 7.

Differences Between E-1 and E-2 Visas

Upfront investment: An E-1 visa does not require an up-front investment, which ultimately makes it much more affordable than an E-2.

Treaty countries: E-1 visas list fewer eligible countries than E-2 visas. Moreover, some countries (like Belgium) have both E-1 and E-2 treaties with the US, whereas other countries only have a treaty for one of the two. For instance, Greece only has an E-1 treaty with the US and not an E-2. Therefore, a citizen of Greece could only apply for an E-1 visa.

Financial risk: With an E-2 visa, the money invested in the enterprise must be at risk and enough to pay for day-to-day business tasks. An E-1 visa does not have any such requirement.

The next section goes into more detail regarding the E-2 Treaty Investor visa.

2. Treaty Investors: E-2

What is an E-2 visa?

An E-2 is a nonimmigrant visa that allows businesspersons from certain countries to work in the US for a business in which they invest. However, E-2 treaty investor visas must not be confused with green cards through investment (EB-5 visa), which will be discussed later in this chapter. Also, while an EB-5 requires a minimum investment of one million dollars, an E-2 visa has no specific dollar minimum set by law.

Key Features of the E-2 Visa

Some of the advantages, disadvantages, and issues regarding the E-2 visa are as follows:

1. The E-2 treaty investor as well as their E-2 employees can work legally in the US for a US business in which a substantial cash investment has been made by the E-2 investor, so long as the investor is a national of a country that has a treaty with the US.

2. While in the US, the E-2 treaty investor or their E-2 employee is restricted to working only for the employer or self-owned business acting as the E-2 visa sponsor.

3. E-2 visas are initially issued for a maximum of two (2) years with unlimited extensions. The length of the visa issuance depends on the reciprocity agreement between the US and the E-2 visa holder's country as well as the viability of the US business (note: new companies tend to receive shorter validity periods).

4. Each time E-2 visa holders re-enter the US, they receive a new period of stay of up to two (2) years. They also may extend their stay while remaining in the US.

5. Visas are available for the accompanying spouse and unmarried children under twenty-one (21) years of age.

6. The accompanying spouse, but not children, is authorized to work in the US by virtue of their E-2 or

E-2S status and does not need to apply for a separate Employment Authorization Document (EAD).

Some people call the E-2 the next best thing to US permanent residence because it is possible to obtain this visa via self-employment, and the status comes with unlimited extensions. Also, there are no annual limits on the number of E-2 visas that can be issued to qualified applicants. A caveat is that once accompanying children reach the age of twenty-one (21), they no longer qualify for any benefits under the E-2 parent's status and must obtain another visa on their own merits to remain in the US.

Qualification Criteria for an E-2 Treaty Investor Visa

There are six (6) requirements for obtaining an E-2 visa:

1. The applicant must be a citizen of either (a) a country with whom the United States maintains a treaty of commerce and navigation, (b) a country with whom the United States maintains a qualifying international agreement, or (c) a country that has been deemed a qualifying country by legislation with the US.
2. The applicant must intend to work in the US for either (a) a company that they own or (b) a company that is at least fifty (50) percent owned by nationals of the applicant's country of origin.
3. The applicant must be either the owner or a "key employee" (executive supervisor or a person with essential skills) of the US business.
4. The applicant or the foreign company must have made a "substantial" investment in the US business. There is

no legal minimum amount to be considered "substantial;" however, the applicant or foreign company must be putting capital or assets at risk and trying to make a profit, and the amount must also be considered substantial relative to the type of business.

5. The US company must be actively engaged in commercial activities and meet the applicable legal requirements for doing business in its state or region. It cannot merely be a means to support the investor. The underlying goal of the treaty investor visa is to create jobs for US workers.

6. The applicant must intend to leave the US when their business in the US is completed, although an E-2 visa holder is not required to maintain a foreign residence abroad. The applicant will likely be asked to show evidence of eventual plans to leave the US during the consular interview.

Sponsoring a Prospective E-2 Employee

Under the E-2 treaty investor nonimmigrant visa category, a US business established by substantial foreign investment and owned at least fifty (50) percent by citizens of an authorized treaty country can temporarily hire workers from that same country to perform executive, supervisory, and essential-skills jobs only. As mentioned previously, the principal investor in such a business can also use this visa category to secure US nonimmigrant status for themselves. Furthermore, the principal investor must be in E-2 status to employ E-2 workers.

Note that the application process is entirely different for a prospective E-2 employee already in the US (in lawful status) than an employee outside the US who needs to apply for an entry visa (do consular processing). Both of these procedures are outlined below.

7. Filing an E-2 Petition for an Employee Already in the US

If a prospective E-2 employee is already in the US (in lawful status), the employer may file a petition with USCIS to change the nonimmigrant status of a prospective employee using Form I-129 (Petition for a Nonimmigrant Worker). This form consists of several pages requesting essential information required for all types of nonimmigrant worker petitions, followed by several sets of additional pages for the specific visa categories. The E supplement, consisting of two (2) pages, requires the employer to set forth the E-2 qualifying characteristics of the business and the prospective employee.

These are the kinds of documents an employer can submit to establish that the business meets the E-2 requirements:

   a. Evidence of possession and control of investment funds such as bank records, financial statements, loans, savings, and promissory notes.
   b. Evidence of remittances of funds to the US such as bank drafts, transfers, exchange permits, and receipts.
   c. Evidence of business establishment in the US such as articles of incorporation, partnership agreements, organizational and staffing charts,

    shares, titles, contracts, receipts, licenses, and leases.

d. Evidence of investors' nationality such as passports, articles of incorporation of the parent company, and stock exchange listings.

e. Evidence of investment in the US such as titles, receipts, contracts, loans, and bank statements.

f. Evidence of the substantiality of the investment such as financial statements, audits, and corporate tax returns.

g. Evidence that the enterprise is not marginal such as payroll records, payroll tax forms, personal tax returns, and other evidence of personal income and assets.

h. Evidence that the enterprise is a real, operating business such as annual reports, catalogs, sales literature, and news articles.

Of course, form instructions only provide general guidance. No list of supporting documents covers all types of E-2 eligible businesses. The documents a business will need to submit will depend on its nature. For instance, a publicly traded corporation might demonstrate the requisite foreign ownership through a stock exchange listing, while a closely held corporation would typically present copies of stock certificates and owners' passport identification pages.

To establish that the business is not marginal, a sole proprietor might present personal income tax returns, proving that the business generates more than enough income to sustain the investor's family. At the same time, a larger company would submit evidence such as payroll records to prove it generates economic activity by employing people.

In addition to documentation qualifying the merits of the business, the petitioner will need to submit evidence that the prospective employee meets the E-2 requirements and is eligible to change status including:

1. Evidence of nationality: Passport identification pages
2. Evidence of current nonimmigrant status: I-94 card (for a description of the I-94 card, see discussion below about maintaining status)
3. Evidence of qualifications: Resume, diplomas, certificates, as relevant

The E-2 petition packet also needs an effective cover letter to assist the USCIS adjudicator in making sense of the documents and understanding how they satisfy the E-2 requirements.

Finally, the I-129 petition must be accompanied by a filing fee of $460. This fee is ordinarily paid by a check or money order made out to the US Department of Homeland Security and submitted in the same package as the petition and supporting materials. Note: A credit card can be used when submitting to a USCIS lockbox, but the I-129 must be sent to a regular USCIS Service Center.

8. E-2 Consular Processing and Reasons to Consider It, Even for Workers Already in the US

USCIS typically grants E-2 status for an initial term of two (2) years. However, if the prospective E-2 hire is contemplating travel outside the US during the first two (2) years of employment, consular processing might make more sense, even when remaining in the US and requesting a change of status is possible.

This is because the employee will need to get a visa at a consular post to re-enter the US after departing and, unlike other types of nonimmigrant petitions, an approved E-2 petition has no force at all at a consular post. For example, an H-1B employee needs only to present an approved, unexpired USCIS petition at a consulate abroad to support the basic visa application form. An E-2 employee, however, will need to make a completely new visa application and present all the required supporting documents in order to be issued a visa. So, why not just go for a visa from the outset?

Maintaining E-2 Status

For applicants who choose to apply from within the US, upon approval of the I-129 petition, USCIS issues an approval notice to the employer that includes a status document. The notice is perforated so that one can tear off the bottom portion (the I-94 card) and give it to the employee to serve as evidence of lawful status. The employer and employee must carefully track the expiration date on the I-94. Typically, E-2 status is granted for an initial two-year term. Applicants who choose to consular process will receive the I-94 card in their passport upon entry to the US.

In both cases, before the I-94 expires, the employer can request to extend the employee's E-2 status by filing a petition for extension with USCIS. Theoretically, E-2 status can be extended an indefinite number of times by filing a petition for an extension every two (2) years. However, USCIS does require supporting evidence for the ongoing need for the foreign employee's services, and employers are frequently asked to present some evidence that no US workers are available for the job in question.

Individuals who processed an E-2 visa abroad will have an alternative way to extend their status, namely simply traveling abroad and re-entering, since the visa itself is typically issued for a five-year term. With each re-entry during the life of the visa, the visa holder should be granted a new two-year period of stay. Thus, through strategic traveling, an E-2 visa holder could convert a five-year visa into a seven-year stay without the need to re-establish their E-2 qualifications—another benefit to choosing consular processing.

3. International Entrepreneur Parole

What is Entrepreneur Parole?

The International Entrepreneur Rule (IER), also referred to as "entrepreneur parole," is a program that allows foreign nationals to be paroled into the US to start a business. The US Department of Homeland Security (DHS) may exercise its parole authority on a case-by-case basis to grant a period of authorized stay to foreign entrepreneurs who can demonstrate that: (1) their presence in the US would provide a "significant public benefit" through their business venture and (2) they deserve a favorable exercise of discretion.

The Entrepreneur Parole program supports entrepreneurs from any industry if they can make a compelling case to the United States Citizenship and Immigration Services (USCIS). The IER is appealing to many candidates due to its openness to a wide spectrum of business areas, especially given that many employment visas have specific industry-related job requirements.

How is Parole Different from a Visa?

Parole is not the same as a visa, and participants in the IER Program do not receive visas. Those who are granted parole are allowed to physically enter the US one (1) time (but are not considered officially "admitted" into the US) and for the sole purpose of developing their business. Should the individual depart and want re-enter to the US, the border official will need to decide whether to grant parole for the remaining time of the authorized parole period.

What are the Requirements for Entrepreneur Parole?

1. The applicant established a US startup within five (5) years prior to the parole application. The startup has conducted business legally since its creation as well as demonstrated immense potential for fast expansion and employment creation.
2. The applicant plays a key and vital role in the startup company and can significantly contribute to the development and success of the company.
3. The applicant, in their capacity as the startup entity's entrepreneur, will bring "significant public benefit" to the US by proving that:

- The investing company has obtained substantial fund investments from competent US investors with a history of profitable investments (a "qualified investment" of at least $311,071 from one (1) or more qualified investors within eighteen (18) months immediately preceding the filing of Form I-941); or
- The startup entity has received considerable grants or awards for research and development, job creation, and/or economic development (or other grants or awards typically given to startup entities) from federal, state, or local government organizations that frequently offer startup entities such grants or awards (the startup must have received at least $124,429 through one (1) or more qualified government awards or grants within eighteen (18) months immediately preceding the filing of Form I-941); or
- The startup can partially satisfy one (1) or both of the above standards as well as offer other credible and convincing proof of the startup entity's significant potential for quick growth and employment creation and, thus, deserves a favorable application of discretion.

Immediate Family Members of Entrepreneur Parolees

The spouse or child of an entrepreneur applying for parole under this rule must demonstrate that they:

- Can independently qualify for parole into the US based on significant public benefit or urgent humanitarian reasons; and

- Deserve a favorable exercise of discretion.

Applying for International Entrepreneur Parole

To apply for Entrepreneur Parole, the applicant needs to complete the following forms as well as provide supporting evidence to prove eligibility.

Form I-941: Application for Entrepreneur Parole

Form I-941 is used for making the initial parole request, asking for additional time, or amending the original application. With this application, the following information and documents must be provided to USCIS as evidence regarding the startup:

- Personal identity information
- Evidence proving the applicant's role in the startup and ownership stake as well as the business's qualifiers for the program
- Documentation that the business meets the "qualified investor" requirements
- Payment for I-941 filing fee ($1,200) and biometrics fee ($85). (Always check the USCIS website to verify current fees).

Form I-131: Application for Travel Document

The main entrepreneur parolee is allowed to apply to bring their spouse and children to the US using Form I-131. One may file this application together with or separately from the initial Form I-941 application. With this form, it is crucial to include proof of relationship to the primary applicant (copies of birth and/or marriage certificates). It must also be shown that the applicant is filing for entrepreneur parole. Note: Canadian nationals are exempted from filing this form.

The current filing fee for Form I-131 is $575 with an additional biometrics service fee of $85.

Form I-765: Application for Employment Authorization

The spouse of the parolee can apply for employment authorization if their Form I-131 is approved. Form I-765 must be submitted only after the entrepreneur has received verified parole.

Form I-9: Employment Eligibility Verification

If the applicant for parole is an employee of the startup, they will also need to submit Form I-9 to the US employer (see Chapter 7 for more information on Form I-9).

Applying for Entrepreneur Parole from a Nonimmigrant Status

Nonimmigrant status holders in the US may apply for the IER program from within the US if their nonimmigrant status is still valid. However, after the parole application is approved, the applicant will need to leave the US and re-enter to receive the parole. They will also lose their nonimmigrant status as one cannot be both an entrepreneur parolee and hold nonimmigrant status at the same time.

If the applicant is in the US but their nonimmigrant status has expired and/or they do not have valid status, they will need to apply for entrepreneur parole from outside of the US. In doing so, however, they run the risk of being denied parole into the US based on their past failure to maintain lawful status in the US.

In all cases, after receiving parole through the IER program, one cannot adjust or change status inside the US. Therefore, if the parolee later becomes eligible for another immigration benefit, they will need to depart the US and obtain the corresponding visa.

Where to File and Processing Times

Completed parole applications should be filed at the USCIS Dallas Lockbox. USCIS has not received sufficient applicants to adequately determine typical processing times for Form I-941. See the USCIS website for the most up-to-date filing and processing time information (uscis.gov).

Extending Entrepreneurial Parole

Upon being paroled into the US, entrepreneurs are granted a stay of thirty (30) months to grow their business. To re-parole after the initial 30-month period, one can re-apply using Form I-941 for an additional thirty (30) months. The IER parole can last up to five (5) years if the applicant remains qualified for parole.

To re-parole, the applicant must provide evidence that:

- The applicant's business/organization still maintains startup qualifications
- The applicant is still qualified as an entrepreneur
- The applicant has retained a minimum five (5) percent ownership interest in the company
- During the initial parole period, the startup:
  - ✓ Created at least five (5) qualified jobs

- ✓ Received a minimum of $622,142 from qualified investors and/or government grants or awards
- ✓ Had a minimum of $622,142 in annual revenue
- ✓ Averaged twenty (20) percent annual revenue growth
- ✓ Provided evidence of potential growth for the future

Termination of Parole

Parole will automatically terminate on the date until which parole was authorized unless an application for re-parole is made. Parole granted under this section may also be automatically terminated if USCIS receives written notice from the entrepreneur parolee that they are no longer employed by the start-up entity or have ceased to possess a qualifying ownership stake in the start-up entity.

Furthermore, the DHS, at its discretion, may terminate parole granted at any time (and with or without prior notice or opportunity to respond) if it determines that the individual's continued parole in the US no longer provides a significant public benefit.

Differences Between Entrepreneur Parole and E-1/E-2 Visas

Nature of the benefit: Whereas E-1 and E-2 are visas, parole is not a visa. Therefore, the eligibility of the entrepreneur will be evaluated each time they enter the US during the parole period.

Treaty country: The main advantage the IER program has over the E-1/E-2 visas is that it is available to foreign nationals from any country, whereas the E-1/E-2 visas are only available to people from E-1/E-2 treaty countries. Thus, the IER Program could be a good alternative if the applicant is not from an E-1 or E-2 treaty county.

Length of authorized stay in the US: One of the main advantages of E-1/E-2 visas over the IER program is the length of time the beneficiary can remain in the US. The IER program is limited to an initial 30-month period with a possible additional thirty (30) months for entrepreneurs who can demonstrate business growth. The E-1/E-2 visas can be renewed an indefinite number of times, provided the business continues to operate successfully.

Required funds amount: The minimum amount required for applying under the IER program is specified, whereas with the E-1 and E-2 visas, there is no mention of any specified amount.

4. Immigrant Investor Program: EB-5

What is an EB-5 visa?

Also known as the "Million Dollar Green Card" or the option to "purchase" a green card, the EB-5 visa can be obtained through the Immigrant Investor Program. This program is particularly appealing to self-employed individuals and company people. The investor green card is an effective way to obtain US permanent residence without waiting extended periods—provided the applicants have enough money or other assets to meet the requirements.

Requirements

The summarized requirements to obtain an EB-5 visa are as follows:

- The applicant must meet established capital investment amount requirements. Typically, an investment of $800,000 or $1,050,000 is required for a US commercial enterprise.
- The investment must create at least ten (10) full-time positions for qualifying employees.
- The business receiving the investment must be eligible for the EB-5 program.

How to Apply

The applicant must file either Form I-526 (Immigrant Petition by Standalone Investor) or Form I-526E (Immigrant Petition by Regional Center Investor).

If an immigrant visa number is immediately available to the applicant, and the applicant is in the US in lawful status, the applicant may file Form I-485 (Application to Register Permanent Residence or Adjust Status) either: a) together with Form I-526 or Form I-526E, b) while Form I-526 or Form I-526E is pending, or c) after Form I-526 or Form I-526E is approved (see below for more details on Form I-485).

Applicants residing outside the US may only file form I-526 or I-526E and, upon approval, consular process an immigrant visa abroad. (See Chapter 7 for more details on consular processing).

Form I-485 Application to Adjust Status in the US (Obtain Green Card)

If in the US in authorized status, the principal applicant and accompanying immediate family members (spouse and unmarried children under twenty-one (21) years of age) must each submit the following documentation and evidence to apply for permanent residence (a green card) as an EB-5 immigrant investor/dependent:

- Form I-485, Application to Register Permanent Residence or Adjust Status;
- Copy of Form I-797, Approval Notice, for I-526/I-526E petition;
- Two passport-style photographs;
- Copy of a government-issued identity document with photograph;
- Copy of birth and marriage certificates (with English translation, if applicable);
- Copy of passport page with nonimmigrant visa (if applicable);
- Copy of passport page with most recent admission or parole stamp (if applicable);
- Copy of Form I-94, Arrival/Departure Record, or the US Customs and Border Protection (CBP) admission or parole stamp on the travel document (if applicable);
- Proof of the applicant's continuous lawful status since arriving in the US;
- Form I-693, Report of Medical Examination and Vaccination Record (depending on the location, it may be required to submit this document together with Form I-485, or it may need to be done at a later time,

such as by mail or in person at the I-485 interview, if any);

- Certified police and court records of criminal charges, arrests, or convictions (if applicable);
- Form I-601, Application for Waiver of Grounds of Inadmissibility (if applicable);
- Form I-212, Application for Permission to Reapply for Admission into the US After Deportation or Removal (if applicable);
- Documentation of past or present J-1 or J-2 nonimmigrant status (if applicable), including proof of either a) compliance with the two-year foreign residence requirement, or b) a waiver of the requirement under INA 212(e);
- Form I-508, Request for Waiver of Certain Rights, Privileges, Exemptions, and Immunities, for applicants who currently hold A, G, or E nonimmigrant status;
- Form I-566, Interagency Record of Request–A, G or NATO Dependent Employment Authorization or Change/Adjustment to/from A, G or NATO Status (only if the applicant has A, G, or NATO nonimmigrant status); and
- Form I-485 Supplement A, Adjustment of Status Under Section 245(i) (if applicable).

Applicants must also submit the corresponding filing fee for each form unless they are exempt or eligible for a fee waiver. See Chapter 7 for additional information regarding adjustment of status processing.

Chapter Two:

Family-Based Immigration

———————— ⊐ ————————

This chapter outlines the various ways that a foreign national can obtain US permanent residence (a green card) through a US citizen or permanent resident family member, including eligibility and documentary requirements, filing steps and procedures, and approximate processing times.

While employers and HR professionals would typically not have much (if any) involvement in these types of immigration cases, it is important to have an overview of all the available options in the event that a current or prospective employee may qualify for one of these benefits.

In some cases, immigrating through a family member can be quite a lengthy process (more than a decade in the case of a sibling petition). However, in other cases, it may prove to be a faster, easier, and less expensive option for the employee (and employer) than an employment-based immigrant visa petition or other immigration avenue.

1. Immigration Visa Processing (IVP): Family-Based Cases

Overview

US citizens and lawful permanent residents (LPRs) are allowed to petition for certain family members to immigrate to the US, granting them permanent residence (a green card) upon their arrival.

Immigrant visa processing (IVP) for family-based petitions involves a series of steps, including filing the appropriate forms, submitting supporting documents, attending interviews, and obtaining an immigrant visa at a US embassy or consulate abroad.

Eligibility Requirements for Family-Based Immigration

As will be detailed in the following sections, the main categories for family-based immigration are as follows:

1. Immediate Relatives (IR):

    - Spouse of a US citizen
    - Unmarried children under twenty-one (21) years of age of a US citizen
    - Parents of a US citizen (petitioner must be at least twenty-one (21) years old)

2. Family Preference Categories:

    - **1st Preference (F1):** Unmarried sons and daughters (over age twenty-one (21)) of US citizens

- **2nd Preference A (F2A):** Spouses and unmarried children (under age twenty-one (21)) of LPRs
- **2nd Preference B (F2B):** Unmarried sons and daughters (over age twenty-one (21)) of LPRs
- **3rd Preference (F3):** Married sons and daughters (of any age) of US citizens
- **4th Preference (F4):** Brothers and sisters of US citizens (petitioner must be at least twenty-one (21) years old)

Required Documents for the IV Application

A family-based immigrant visa application requires a comprehensive set of required documents including:

- Passport(s) for the beneficiary and any accompanying family members.
- Birth certificate(s) for the beneficiary and any accompanying family members.
- Marriage certificate (if applicable).
- Divorce or death certificates for any prior marriages (if applicable).
- Proof of the petitioner's US citizenship or LPR status.
- Proof of financial support (e.g., Form I-864, recent tax return, W-2, paystubs, employment verification letter).
- Police clearance certificates from all countries beneficiaries aged sixteen (16) or older have lived in for six (6) months or longer.
- Digital passport-sized photographs.

Family-Based Immigration Process

Petitioning for a family member to immigrate to the US involves several steps, including but not limited to:

1. Filing Form I-130 with USCIS to establish the qualifying relationship (for more details, see Chapter 4).
2. Waiting for USCIS approval and visa availability (for preference categories).
3. Submitting required documents and attending visa interview at the US consulate.
4. Receiving the immigrant visa packet.
5. Entering the US with an immigrant visa.
6. Receiving the green card by mail after arrival in the US.

Please note that processing times may vary based on factors such as the applicant's country of origin and the family-based visa category.

Conclusion

Family-based immigrant visas play a vital role in reuniting families and enabling eligible individuals to obtain permanent residency in the US. This overview outlines the basics of the family-based immigrant visa process, however navigating the immigration system alone can be complex and overwhelming. While not required, hiring an immigration law professional can simplify the process for individuals and their family members and ensure the best and most efficient outcomes.

2. Immigrant Petition for Spouses and Children

Overview

The I-130 form, also known as the "Petition for Alien Relative," is the first step in the family-based green card process for qualified relatives of a US citizen (USC) or US lawful permanent resident (LPR). This petition, together with its accompanying documentation, is essential for establishing the familial relationship between the petitioner and the beneficiary.

This section covers the basics of the I-130 petition specifically for spouses and children including eligibility criteria, requirements, and the necessary documents the petitioner and beneficiary must present. Additionally, some common questions regarding the petition process will be answered.

Eligibility (Spouses and Children)

A US citizen may submit an immigrant visa petition for their:

- Spouse
- Child of any age (married or unmarried)

A US lawful permanent resident may only submit an immigrant visa petition for their:

- Spouse
- Unmarried child of any age

Requirements for the I-130 Petition for a Spouse or Child

When filing the I-130 petition for a spouse or child, the petitioner must adhere to the following requirements:

- Accurately complete Form I-130.
- Pay the required filing fee.
- Provide evidence of the petitioner's US citizenship or lawful permanent resident status.
- Provide sufficient documentation to establish the qualifying familial relationship to the beneficiary.

Required Documents

The I-130 petition must be accompanied by specific documentation from both the petitioner and the beneficiary. Any documents not in English must be accompanied by a certified English translation.

From the petitioner:

- Proof of US citizenship or permanent resident status.
- A copy of their birth certificate and passport.
- A copy of their marriage certificate.
- Proof of legal termination of prior marriages (if applicable).

From the beneficiary:

- A copy of their passport.
- A copy of their birth certificate.
- Proof of legal termination of prior marriages (if applicable).

- If the beneficiary is a spouse, additional proof of the marital relationship (e.g., joint accounts and other documents, timeline of relationship, photographs together at different times and places).

Application Process

The USC or LPR petitioner must file Form I-130, Petition for Alien Relative, with USCIS. The petitioner may either fill out the form online or download, print, and mail it to one of the USCIS processing centers in Chicago, Dallas, Phoenix, or the Elgin Lockbox along with the required supporting documents and filing fee.

If there is a visa number immediately available to the beneficiary and the beneficiary is already in the US, then the beneficiary can simultaneously file Form I-485, Application for Adjustment of Status, to become a lawful permanent resident. If the beneficiary is outside the US, they will need to immigrant visa process (IVP). See Chapter 7 for more detailed information on adjustment of status (Form I-485) and immigrant visa processing (IVP).

If there is not a visa number immediately available to the beneficiary (as in the case of relatives of lawful permanent residents and adult children of US citizens), the approved I-130 petition will secure a place in the cue (establish a "priority date") for the beneficiary. However, the beneficiary will need to wait until their priority date is current to receive their green card, either via adjustment of status or immigrant visa processing. In some cases, this wait time can be several years or even over a decade, depending on the visa category and the beneficiary's country of origin.

In the case of spouses and minor children of lawful permanent residents, this wait time can be significantly reduced or eliminated altogether if the petitioner becomes a US citizen (see section on Application for Naturalization).

Conclusion

The I-130 application for spouses or children is a crucial first step in the family-based green card process. It is essential to provide accurate and complete information and supporting documents to avoid delays or denials.

Special Questions and FAQ

Can a parent petition for an adopted child?

A: Yes, a USC or LPR can petition for an adopted child if the adoption took place before the child turned sixteen (16) years of age. Sufficient legal documentation of the adoption must be provided.

Can a parent petition for a stepchild?

A: Yes, a USC or LPR can petition for a stepchild. However, the marriage creating the stepparent-stepchild relationship must have occurred before the child turned eighteen (18) years of age. Proof of the qualifying marriage, such as marriage/divorce certificates, and evidence of the stepchild-stepparent relationship, must be included.

3. Immigrant Petition for Parents

Overview

This section covers the basics of the I-130 petition specifically for a parent of a US citizen including eligibility criteria, requirements, and the necessary documents the petitioner and beneficiary must present. A parent of a US citizen is considered an "immediate relative" in the sense that an immigrant visa number is always immediately available to beneficiaries in this category.

Eligibility

To file an I-130 petition for a parent, the petitioner must meet the following criteria:

- Be a US citizen.
- Be at least twenty-one (21) years old.

Note: Only US citizens may file immigrant petitions for their parents. If a US lawful permanent wishes to petition for a parent, the LPR will first need to complete the process of naturalization to become a US citizen (see Chapter 7 for more information about the naturalization process).

Requirements for the I-130 Petition for a Parent

When filing an I-130 petition for a parent, the petitioner must adhere to the following requirements:

- Accurately complete Form I-130.
- Pay the required filing fee.
- Provide evidence of their US citizenship.

- Establish the qualifying parent-child relationship through appropriate documentation.

Required Documents

The I-130 petition must be accompanied by specific documentation from both the petitioner and the parent beneficiary. Any documents not in English must be accompanied by a certified English translation.

From the petitioner:

- Proof of US citizenship.
- A copy of their birth certificate or passport.
- A copy of their marriage certificate (if applicable).
- Proof of the parent-child relationship (e.g., birth certificate).

From the parent beneficiary:

- A copy of their passport.
- A copy of their birth certificate.
- Proof of current and every prior marriage, divorce, or widow(er) status.

Application Process

The US citizen petitioner must file Form I-130, Petition for Alien Relative, on their parent's behalf with USCIS. If the parent is already in the US, then the parent can simultaneously file Form I-485, Application for Adjustment of Status, as parents of US citizens do not need to wait for a visa number to become available to apply for a green card. See Chapter 7 for additional information on the adjustment of status process.

If the beneficiary is outside the US, they will need to immigrant visa process (IVP) through a US embassy or consulate. See Chapter 7 for more detailed information on family-based immigrant visa processing (IVP).

Special Questions and FAQ

Can adopted children apply for their parents?

A: Yes, adopted children over the age of twenty-one (21) who meet the eligibility criteria can file an I-130 petition for their adoptive parents if the adoption took place before the petitioner turned sixteen (16) years of age. Sufficient legal documentation of the adoption must be provided.

Is it possible to petition for a stepparent?

A: Yes, US citizens over the age of twenty-one (21) can sponsor their stepparents if the marriage creating the stepparent relationship occurred before the petitioner turned eighteen (18) years of age. Proof of the qualifying marriage, such as marriage/divorce certificates, and evidence of the stepchild-stepparent relationship, must be included.

Are there any other special circumstances for parents?

A: Yes, there are other scenarios, such as cases involving widows/widowers of US citizens, parents of US citizens serving in the military, and others. Each situation has specific requirements. Parents of US citizens may also be eligible for a green card on humanitarian grounds, such as if they are facing persecution in their home country.

4. Immigrant Petition for Siblings

Overview

A sibling green card, officially known as the Family-Sponsored Fourth Preference (F4) Immigrant Visa, is an immigrant visa category that allows US citizens to petition for their brothers and sisters for US permanent residence (a green card).

Eligibility

To file an I-130 immigrant petition for a sibling, the petitioner must meet the following criteria:

- Be a US citizen.
- Be at least twenty-one (21) years old.

Process

1. I-130 Petition:

The US citizen (petitioner) must file an immigrant visa petition on behalf of their foreign national sibling (beneficiary) using Form I-130, Petition for Alien Relative.

The I-130 petition must be accompanied by specific documentation from both the petitioner and the sibling beneficiary. Any documents not in English must be accompanied by a certified English translation.

From the petitioner:

- Proof of US citizenship.
- A copy of their birth certificate.
- A copy of their marriage certificate (if applicable).

- Proof of the sibling relationship (e.g., birth certificates showing same parent(s), marriage certificate of parents).

From the sibling beneficiary:

- A copy of their passport.
- A copy of their birth certificate.
- Proof of current and every prior marriage, divorce, or widow(er) status.

2. Waiting Period:

One of the most significant challenges with the sibling green card category is the lengthy waiting period. This category has a limited number of visas available each year, and demand typically exceeds supply. As a result, beneficiaries may have to wait for several years, or even decades, before an immigrant visa becomes available for them.

3. Immigrant Visa or Adjustment of Status Application:

Once an immigrant visa number becomes available, the beneficiary will be notified by the National Visa Center (NVC) and may apply for an immigrant visa at a US consulate or embassy in their home country. If the beneficiary is already in the US, they may be able to apply for a green card in the US through a process known as adjustment of status (see Chapter 7 for more details on the adjustment of status process).

Required Documentation

The immigrant visa or adjustment of status application requires specific documentation from both the petitioner and the beneficiary, namely:

- Immigrant visa petition approval notice (Form I-797)
- Proof of the petitioner's US citizenship (US passport, Naturalization Certificate, US birth certificate, etc.)
- Valid passport (both petitioner and beneficiary)
- Police certificates (only for consular processing)
- Medical examination results (if applicable)
- Affidavit of Support (Form I-864)
- Petitioner's or joint sponsor's financial documents (e.g., tax returns, W-2s, pay stubs, etc.)
- Proof of sibling relationship (birth certificates, parents' marriage certificate, etc.)

4. Interview and Medical Examination:

Whether the beneficiary consular processes or applies to adjust status from within the US, they will typically need to attend a personal interview and also undergo a medical examination by an approved panel physician. Usually, a decision on the application is given at the end of the interview or shortly thereafter.

5. Visa Issuance:

If the beneficiary's visa application is approved, they will receive an immigrant visa sticker in their passport, allowing them to travel to and reside in the US as a permanent resident.

6. Entry to the US:

Upon arrival in the US, they will be inspected by US Customs and Border Protection (CBP) and officially admitted as US permanent residents. A physical "green card" will be mailed to the US address they provide within a few weeks.

Conclusion

Once granted permanent residency, siblings have the right to live and work in the US indefinitely. They are also eligible for various government benefits but are expected to abide by US laws and tax regulations.

Special Questions and FAQ

Is it possible to petition for stepsiblings?

A: Yes, US citizens can sponsor their stepsiblings if the marriage of their parents creating the stepsibling relationship occurred before both turned eighteen (18) years old. Proof of the qualifying marriage, such as marriage/divorce certificates and evidence of the stepsibling relationship must be included.

Is it possible to petition for an adopted sibling?

A: Yes, a US citizen can petition for an adopted sibling if the adoption took place before the beneficiary turned sixteen (16) years old. Sufficient legal documentation of the adoption must be provided.

Is it possible to petition for a half-sibling?

A: Yes, US citizens can sponsor a half-sibling. If the petitioner and beneficiary share the same mother, then only the standard documentation listed above is necessary to prove the sibling relationship (birth certificates of the siblings listing the same mother). If the petitionary and beneficiary share only the same father, then marriage certificates showing the relationship of each of the siblings' mothers with the shared father are also required.

5. Nonimmigrant Visa for Fiancé(e)s (K-1)

Overview

A US citizen can also petition for their foreign national fiancé(e) living outside the US to join them in the US. This is called a K-1 nonimmigrant visa, and the sole purpose is for the sponsored fiancé(e) to enter the US, marry the petitioner within ninety (90) days, and apply for US lawful permanent residence as the spouse of a US citizen.

Basics of a K-1 Petition for Fiancé(e)

The K-1 nonimmigrant visa is for the foreign national fiancé(e) of a US citizen. Also, children of an eligible fiancé(e) can be granted a K-2 visa.

The US citizen petitioner must first file a Form I-129, Petition for Alien Fiancé(e), with USCIS. The petitioner and beneficiary must have been legally free to marry when the petition was filed and must remain so after that until the date of their marriage. A marriage between the couple must also be legally possible according to the laws of the US state in which the marriage is planned to take place.

Eligibility for K-1 Visa

1. The petitioner must be a US citizen. A US lawful permanent resident is not permitted to sponsor their fiancé(e) for a K-1 visa.
2. Each partner must be unmarried.
3. The couple must prove they met in person at least once within the two (2) years immediately preceding the visa application. This requirement might be

waived in cases of extreme hardship or where meeting in person would violate certain religious, cultural, or social norms.

4. The couple must get legally married within ninety (90) days of the beneficiary arriving in the US.
5. The petitioner must meet the income requirements according to the Federal Poverty Guidelines for a K-1 visa. If the petitioner does not reach the income requirement, they must obtain a joint sponsor.

Step-by-Step Process to Obtain a K-1 Visa

Step 1: First, the US citizen petitioner must file Form I-129F, Petition for Alien Fiancé(e), with USCIS. This form aims to prove the relationship is valid. Once the form and supporting documents are filed at the appropriate address, USCIS will typically send a receipt notice within thirty (30) days. Once the petition is approved, USCIS will send an approval notice.

Step 2: After USCIS approves the petition, the file is sent to the National Visa Center (NVC). The NVC will give the file a case number and send it to the corresponding US embassy or consulate in the beneficiary's home country or country of residence.

Step 3: The beneficiary must then complete the State Department's online Form DS-160 ("Online Nonimmigrant Visa Application"). This is the actual K-1 visa application, and it is crucial to print the confirmation page once the form has been submitted online.

Step 4: A visa interview will be scheduled at the nearest US embassy or consulate in the beneficiary's home country or country of residence, usually about four (4) to six (6) weeks after the embassy's initial notice. The interviewing officer will typically decide on the case either on the day of the interview or shortly afterward. If additional evidence is needed, they will request it to be submitted directly to the US consulate or embassy.

Step 5: Once the visa is approved, the foreign fiancé(e) can use it to apply for a single admission at any US port of entry within the validity period of the visa—which will be a maximum of six (6) months from the date of issuance. Upon arrival, the couple must marry within ninety (90) days, or the sponsored fiancé(e) will lose K-1 status. If the couple decides not to get married, the sponsored partner will no longer be eligible to remain in the US and must leave the country immediately.

Step 6: Once the couple has married, the K-1 visa holder can apply for an adjustment of status to lawful permanent resident (see Chapter 7 for more details on the adjustment of status process).

Required Documents

For Form I-129F:

- Proof that the petitioner is a US citizen (US passport, certificate of naturalization, or US birth certificate).
- Copy of the beneficiary's passport.
- Evidence proving the relationship is bona fide such as pictures together, travel itineraries for trips taken together, letters from family and friends confirming the relationship, emails or text messages between the partners, etc.
- Evidence that the couple has met in person at least once within the two (2) years prior to submitting the

petition. Evidence can include flight bookings, hotel itineraries, pictures, emails, etc.

- A sworn statement from each partner explaining the nature of their relationship and stating they intend to get married within ninety (90) days after the beneficiary arrives in the US.
- Copies of all Form I-94 arrival/departure records previously issued to the beneficiary (if any).
- One (1) passport-style photo of the petitioner and one (1) passport-style photo of the beneficiary.
- Evidence that any prior marriages of the petitioner and/or beneficiary have been terminated and that the couple is free to marry each other (if applicable).

For Form DS-160:

Beneficiary's Documents:

- Two passport-style photos
- Birth certificate
- Valid, unexpired passport
- Police clearance obtained from all countries where the beneficiary has resided for more than six (6) months since the age of sixteen (16)
- Sealed, completed medical exam form (obtained through a physician abroad authorized by the State Department)

Petitioner's Documents:

- Affidavit of Support (Form I-134)
- Financial Documents (tax returns, W-2s, pay stubs, etc.)

- Proof of bona fide relationship (copy of the approved I-129F package originally filed with USCIS)

Some Important Points to Remember

K-1 and K-2 (dependent child of a K-1) visa status is temporary. Therefore, the marriage must occur within ninety (90) days of entering the US. Working in the US while on a K-1 visa is allowed. However, the work authorization remains valid only for ninety (90) days. Also, K-1 visa holders cannot change to another nonimmigrant status (for example, F-1 student or H-1B employee). If the couple decides not to marry, the foreign national must leave the US, obtain a new visa, and re-enter with the new visa.

Conclusion

The K-1 visa is unique. While the initial period of admission to the US is relatively short and has certain restrictions, it is an extraordinary way to bypass the lengthy consular processing times of an immigrant petition for a spouse and unite the couple beginning a new life together in the US much faster.

Chapter Three:

Humanitarian Applications

I n addition to student, employment, investment, and family-based immigration avenues, the US offers a variety of short and long-term immigration benefits to foreign nationals facing humanitarian crises in their home country or in the US. New programs are being added and existing programs modified or ended as conditions around the world may improve or worsen.

While these types of benefits do not typically require participation by a US employer or an HR professional, it is important to be aware of these programs as a current or future employee may be or become eligible for a benefit as situations change. Additionally, new employees who present to work with an employment authorization document (EAD) often obtained the EAD as a result of a pending humanitarian application.

In some cases, a humanitarian program may provide a faster and more viable path to obtaining work authorization and, ultimately, permanent residence than an employer petition. In other cases, the relief may only be temporary, and if the employer wishes to maintain the individual on staff, an employment-based petition or other solution may be needed.

1. Filing for Asylum: Affirmative and Defensive Processes

Overview

People from all over the world come to the US each year seeking protection from persecution they have suffered or fear they will suffer due to:

- Race
- Religion
- Nationality
- Membership in a particular social group
- Political opinion

A person in one of these situations may file an asylum application only if they are physically present in the US and are not US citizens or lawful permanent residents. Asylum application was made possible by UN General Assembly Resolution 429 (V), adopted in 1950.

An asylum application can be made **affirmatively** (before removal proceedings are initiated) and/or **defensively** (as a defense to removal proceedings in an immigration court). Each process is outlined in detail below.

Affirmative Asylum Process

The following steps explain how to apply for asylum in the US through the affirmative asylum process.

1. Arrival in the US: The first step is to arrive in the US legally. Individuals who illegally enter the US through its southern land border or adjacent coastal borders will be presumed ineligible for asylum effective May 11, 2023, unless they can demonstrate an exception to the norm or refute the presumption.

2. Submission of Asylum Application: The second step is to apply with US Citizenship and Immigration Services (USCIS) using Form I-589, Application for Asylum and Withholding of Removal, within one (1) year of last arrival in the US (unless the applicant qualifies for an exception to the one-year filing deadline). Under Section 208(a)(2)(B) of the Immigration and Nationality Act (INA), an individual may not be eligible to apply for asylum if they fail to file Form I-589 within one (1) year of their most recent arrival in the US.

Once USCIS receives the completed application, the applicant will be mailed two (2) notices:

- An acknowledgment of receipt of the application, and
- A notice to go to the nearest Application Support Center (ASC) for fingerprinting.

3. Fingerprinting and Background Checks: The applicant must then appear for a fingerprinting appointment at an ASC. For asylum applicants, there is no fingerprinting fee. Applicants who include their spouse and children in the US on their asylum application must accompany their family members to their ASC appointment. After the fingerprinting is completed, background/security checks will be run on all applicants.

4. Employment Authorization: For individuals who filed for asylum on or after January 4, 1995, the wait time before they may submit a request for employment authorization (Form 1-765) is one hundred and fifty (150) days. Furthermore, USCIS cannot grant employment authorization until an additional thirty (30) days have elapsed after this time, resulting in a total waiting period of one hundred and eighty (180) days. It is essential to note that the 180-day Asylum EAD Clock does not account for any delays that applicants may cause or request while their applications are under review with an asylum office or immigration court.

5. Notice of Asylum Interview: In the next step, the applicant will receive notice for an interview with a USCIS asylum officer at either an asylum office or a field office, depending on the applicant's location. The notice will contain the date, time, and location of the asylum interview.

6. Interview: On the interview day, the applicant, the applicant's spouse, and any children seeking derivative benefits must be present at the interview. The applicant can also bring an attorney to the interview if desired, however, the applicant must have an interpreter if they are unable to speak English during the interview. In addition, they may bring witnesses to testify on their behalf. An interview generally lasts an hour; however, the length may vary from case to case.

7. Adjudication: After the interview, the asylum officer will evaluate eligibility and make a preliminary decision, which a supervisory asylum officer must review. Supervisory asylum officers may refer a preliminary decision to USCIS headquarters for additional review based on the specific circumstances of the case.

8. Decision: Asylum applicants usually return to the asylum office about two (2) weeks after the interview to pick up their decision. Application processing may take longer if:

- The applicant currently holds a valid immigration status.
- The interview took place at a USCIS field office.
- The security checks are still in process.
- The case is pending review by the asylum staff at USCIS headquarters.

In the event the asylum application is denied by the Asylum Office and the applicant does not have lawful status, the applicant will receive a referral letter explaining why they were denied asylum together with a Notice to Appear in Immigration Court (NTA). See "Defensive Asylum Process" (below) for information about applying or re-applying for asylum in Immigration Court.

Defensive Asylum Process

During the defensive asylum process, a foreign national is in immigration proceedings (immigration court) and must prove to an immigration judge that they have a well-founded fear that they would be persecuted upon return to their country of origin. The individual may or may not have already submitted an affirmative asylum application to USCIS that was denied.

Steps in the Defensive Asylum Process

1. Master Calendar Hearing (MCH)

In Immigration Court, there are two (2) types of court dates: the Master Calendar Hearing (MCH) and the Individual Hearing (IH). For the MCH, the foreign national will receive a Notice to Appear (NTA), also known as Form I-862. At the top right of the NTA is the individual's A-Number, an eight

(8) or nine (9) digit immigration identification number that begins with the letter A. This number can be used to consult the immigration court website (https://acis.eoir.justice.gov/en/) for information regarding the date(s) of upcoming hearings and other pertinent information.

The first court date listed on the Notice to Appear (NTA) will be the Master Calendar Hearing (MCH). In MCH proceedings, the Immigration Judge (IJ) is responsible for dealing with administrative issues, including scheduling, application filing, pleadings to immigration charges, and other situations that may arise. Generally, twenty (20) to thirty (30) respondents are scheduled for an MCH within a span of two (2) hours. Most IJs will choose to hear cases in which the respondents are represented by lawyers first. Some IJs will hear "pro bono" cases (lawyers working free of charge) before hearing cases involving private attorneys.

1.1 Arriving in Court

For individuals who hire an attorney (whether pro bono or private), a completed Form EOIR-28, Notice of Entry of Appearance as Attorney of Representative Before Immigration Court, must be submitted to the IJ and the Immigration and Customs Enforcement (ICE) attorney before or on the date of the first MCH at which the individual's attorney will appear. Even if the attorney had previously represented the individual with an asylum application before the Asylum Office, it is still necessary for an attorney to submit an EOIR-28 to become the attorney of record for removal proceedings.

1.2 Beginning of the Hearing

The IJ will most likely discuss the case off the record with each respondent to determine their intentions and resolve any procedural issues. On the record, the IJ will ask respondents if they understand the nature of the proceedings and if they have an attorney to represent them. IJs usually ask individuals without counsel if they wish to have additional time to seek legal representation. It is highly recommended that individuals in immigration proceedings—especially those planning on asking for asylum—seek legal representation due to the complexity of these cases.

1.3 Establishing Receipt of the NTA

The attorney or respondent will then be asked if the respondent received a physical copy of the NTA. If the respondent did not receive it, they should inform the court immediately and ask for a copy. In this case, the IJ usually grants a continuance so the attorney can examine the NTA with the respondent to determine if the charges are accurate. If there is even the slightest doubt about the accuracy of the charges, a continuance should be requested.

1.4 Admitting or Denying the Charges and Conceding Removability

During the MCH, the respondent or their counsel will be required to admit or deny the accuracy of the allegations in the NTA.

1.5 Designating a Country of Removal and Client's Desire to Apply for Asylum

The IJ will then ask the respondent if a country of removal should be designated. The respondent or their attorney should inform the IJ that the respondent does not wish to designate a country of removal, and, by default, the IJ will then establish the respondent's country of origin as the country of removal. At that time, a statement will be made for the record by the attorney or the respondent that the respondent wishes to seek asylum.

It is also essential to request any other alternative grounds for relief from removal at that time, such as Withholding of Removal, Convention Against Torture (CAT), and/or Voluntary Departure (VD).

Some common forms of relief from removal are:

- **Withholding of Removal:** Similar to asylum but with a higher standard of proof, it prevents removal to a country where the individual's life or freedom would be threatened based on race, religion, nationality, political opinion, or membership in a particular social group.
- **Convention Against Torture (CAT):** Prevents removal to a country where the individual would more likely than not face torture by or with the consent of a public official.
- **Cancellation of Removal:** A discretionary form of relief that allows certain foreign nationals who have been living in the US for a long time and have good moral character to avoid removal if they can show that

their removal would cause exceptional and extremely unusual hardship to their US citizen or lawful permanent resident spouse, parent, or child.

- **Adjustment of Status:** Allows certain persons eligible for an immigrant visa (such as through family or employment) to change their status from nonimmigrant to lawful permanent resident (green card holder) without leaving the US.
- **Waivers:** Exceptions that allow certain persons who are otherwise removable due to specific grounds (such as criminal convictions or fraud) to remain in the US if they can show that they deserve a favorable exercise of discretion by the immigration judge.

1.6 Setting a Date for Submission of the Asylum Application

If the respondent has not yet submitted a written asylum application, the IJ will usually set a deadline to do so, which is approximately thirty (30) to forty-five (45) days. However, in the event the respondent's attorney is working pro bono and has a full caseload, the IJ may grant closer to forty-five (45) days.

1.7 Requesting an Interpreter

The IJ will also ask the respondent (or their attorney) which language is most appropriate for the respondent. The court will provide a professional interpreter for the Individual Hearing (IH). Note: Respondents are generally not allowed to provide their own interpreter for an IH.

1.8 Setting an IH (Merits Hearing) Date and Time

An IH (a hearing on the merits of the claim) will usually be scheduled to take place several months (or more) later. The IJ may ask how many hours it will take to complete the IH, and the respondent or their attorney should request at least three (3) to four (4) hours. The MCH is adjourned once the next hearing date has been set.

1.9 Filing for Asylum with the Immigration Court

If the respondent had not previously applied for affirmative asylum, they must submit the asylum application and supporting materials by the deadline given by the Immigration Judge at the Master Calendar Hearing.

Asylum application filing rules and procedures (in immigration court):

- Respondents who are filing Form I-589, Application for Asylum and Withholding of Removal, for the first time must do so within one (1) year of entering the US.
- Respondents must also include a Certificate of Service (COS) with all supporting documents. This certificate is a brief form that shows that the submission was shared with the US Department of Homeland Security (DHS) trial attorney.
- An application may be submitted by mail, using a courier service, dropping it off at the court window, or handing it in at the MCH.

If the respondent already filed a prior asylum application that was denied, they may want to upgrade it. To do this, they must:

1. File an amended Form I-589, and
2. Submit any additional supporting documents or witness statements for the immigration judge to consider. It is crucial to ensure that the information submitted on the amended I-589 is consistent with the previous submission to avoid credibility issues.

In both of these cases, having a good lawyer increases the chances of obtaining asylum. Typically, attorneys would also include a legal brief outlining the most vital legal elements of the claim.

Also, prior to the filing deadline for the asylum application, a list of witnesses, the amount of time needed to testify, and the language the witnesses speak must be submitted.

1.10 Background Checks

Prior to the IH, biometric fingerprints of the respondent will be taken, and background/security checks will be run.

1.11 Preparing for the Individual Hearing (IH)

While there is no guarantee that the respondent will win their case at the Individual Hearing, there are some things respondents can do before and during the hearing to improve their chances:

- Hire an experienced immigration attorney to advise them of their options, prepare their case, and represent them at the hearing.
- Review the case carefully and understand the legal basis for the charges of removal and the forms of relief as well as what types of evidence need to be presented to prove eligibility for the requested relief.

- Gather all the documents that support the case and organize them in a clear, logical manner. Each document should be labeled with an exhibit number, and the respondent (or their lawyer) must provide copies to the IJ and ICE attorney at least fifteen (15) days before the hearing date. A summarized list of exhibits and their relevance to the case should also be prepared.

- Prepare the witnesses and themselves for testimony. Each witness should be prepared with the questions they may be asked and how to answer them truthfully and persuasively. The respondent should also prepare and practice their own testimony and anticipate any questions or challenges from the IJ or the government attorney.

- During the hearing, be honest and consistent with their statements and evidence. Do not lie or exaggerate anything that could hurt their credibility or expose them to further charges.

- Be respectful and cooperative with the immigration judge and the government attorney. Do not argue or interrupt them unnecessarily. Listen carefully to their questions and answer them directly and politely.

- Be confident and persuasive with their arguments. Explain why they deserve relief from removal and why the immigration judge should grant it.

The Individual Hearing before the immigration court is a crucial step in any removal proceedings. It is where an individual can present their case in detail and convince an immigration judge to let them stay in the US. However, it is also a complex and challenging process that requires careful preparation and, preferably, legal representation.

2. The Individual Hearing (IH)

Individual (or Merits) Hearings are formal, adversarial, evidentiary proceedings conducted on the record. Asylum applicants (respondents) are examined by ICE attorneys who serve as prosecutors to disprove the respondent's eligibility for asylum. Each witness is sworn in, and both sides can cross-examine each other. IJs usually also question the respondent.

2.1 Rules of Procedure

An immigration court merits hearing is like any administrative law hearing conducted by other federal or state agencies. However, immigration proceedings are not governed by the Administrative Procedure Act (APA), so the rules of procedure are generally less formal.

2.2 Rules of Evidence

Rules of evidence in asylum hearings are minimal and very casually observed. In most cases, no formal presentation of evidence is required. In most cases, IJs will accept documents or physical evidence without requiring formal authentication, although they may allow argument.

2.3 Before the Beginning of Formal Testimony

A significant amount of off-the-record discussion takes place before an IH, during which the IJ reviews the file, identifies exhibits, and clarifies issues, such as the status of previously filed motions and the number of witnesses the respondent will call. The IJ also ensures that all evidence submitted is appropriately entered into the record. Additionally, an attorney may update or correct information concerning the asylum application or other materials before going on record.

It is also common for the IJ to hold a conference with the respondent's attorney and the ICE attorney rather than proceeding directly to the hearing. The IJ may also request that the two attorneys discuss the case before going on record to see whether any agreement can be reached.

2.4 Opening Statements

Some IJs may permit opening statements, while others may not. In some cases, attorneys cannot give them if a pre-hearing memorandum has been filed.

2.5 Examination of Witnesses

The examination of witnesses is generally the same as that conducted in most other courts. First, the respondent's attorney presents their case, followed by a cross-examination by the ICE attorney and, subsequently, a redirect examination if necessary.

2.6 Direct Examination and Cross-Examination

The direct examination should be well-prepared by both attorneys, and the respondent should be well-rehearsed on what to say. If the respondent cannot answer a question correctly, they should state this clearly and succinctly without engaging in long narratives. Following direct examination, the ICE attorney will conduct a cross-examination, focusing on credibility. Although there are no rules of procedure or evidence, the respondent's attorney may raise objections if the questions are inappropriate.

2.7 Examination by the Immigration Judge

Following the attorneys' direct and cross-examinations, the IJ will conduct an extensive examination. In some cases, the IJ may also interrupt the direct or cross-examination on several occasions, thus disrupting the flow of questions and creating a sense of apprehension on the respondent's part.

2.8 Closing Statements

Before reaching a decision, most IJs allow both sides to make a closing statement.

2.9 The Decision of the Immigration Judge

In most cases, the IJ will issue an oral decision on the same day as the hearing. The IJ will sometimes send the respondent a written decision by mail or schedule a Master Calendar Hearing (MCH) date for them to return for the decision, especially when there is a complex or novel issue of law. However, these incidents are rare.

2.10 Reserving/Waiving Appeal Rights

After reading their decision, the IJ will ask the respondent's and ICE attorneys if they reserve or waive their right to appeal. In the event of an unfavorable decision, respondents usually reserve the right to appeal. The IJ will then provide both attorneys with preprinted order forms stating the relief granted (if any) and whether appeal rights have been reserved. If the respondent receives a favorable decision, this form may be their only proof of immigration status until they are issued a new I-94 or employment authorization document.

It is important to note that, if the respondent loses the case and chooses to appeal, they must submit the papers to the Board of Immigration Appeals (BIA) within thirty (30) days of the decision. Otherwise, the right to appeal is automatically lost.

3. Appeals Process

3.1 Board of Immigration Appeals (BIA)

The BIA generally does not conduct courtroom proceedings to decide appealed cases. Rather, it conducts a "paper review" of cases and issues a decision. On rare occasions, the BIA will hear oral arguments on appealed cases, usually at their headquarters in Falls Church, Virginia.

3.2 US Circuit Court of Appeals

If the BIA denies the asylum appeal, the next possible step is to file an appeal with the US Circuit Court of Appeals (a federal court) serving the region of the US where the respondent lives. The respondent (or their attorney) will need to submit a written statement (legal brief) explaining why the BIA's decision was wrong or an abuse of discretion.

3.3 US Supreme Court

If the case is again denied, there is one last possible avenue of relief—the US Supreme Court. The respondent's attorney must send a petition for a "writ of certiorari." However, the Supreme Court is not obligated to take every case and chooses to review and hear only a limited number of cases each year. The respondent may remain legally in the US during the entire appeals process.

2. Victims of Human Trafficking: T Visa

Overview

The T category is a nonimmigrant visa that is issued specifically to the victims and immediate family members of the victims of human trafficking. Here, the term "human trafficking" denotes both "sex trafficking" and "labor trafficking."

The T visa is a special immigration relief introduced by the Victims of Trafficking and Violence Protection Act (VTVPA) of 2000. T status allows holders to stay in the US for an initial period of up to four (4) years, which can later be extended. Also, its holders are eligible to apply for lawful permanent residence (a green card) after three (3) years of continuous physical presence in the US.

One caveat is that the total number of persons who may be issued T visas or otherwise granted nonimmigrant T status during a fiscal year may not exceed five thousand (5,000). This numerical limitation (or "cap") only counts visas granted to principal applicants and not to their accompanying immediate family members.

Who is Eligible for a T Visa?

To be eligible for a T visa, applicants must meet the following conditions outlined in Sections 103 and 107 of the VPVTA of 2000:

1. The applicant is or was a victim of a "severe form of trafficking persons" as defined in Section 103 of the VPVTA. Accordingly, "severe form of trafficking

persons" encompasses two meanings. The first meaning includes sex trafficking, in which a commercial sex act is induced by force, fraud, coercion, or in which the victim has not attained eighteen (18) years of age. The second meaning denotes labor trafficking, wherein any sort of labor using force, fraud, or coercion is perpetuated for subjection to involuntary servitude, peonage, debt bondage, or slavery.

2. The applicant is physically present in the US, American Samoa, the Commonwealth of the Northern Mariana Islands, or at a port of entry as a direct result of trafficking.

3. The applicant has complied with any reasonable request for assistance in the investigation or prosecution of acts of trafficking. This requirement is excused if the applicant was under the age of eighteen (18) at the time at least one (1) of the acts of trafficking occurred or if the applicant is unable to cooperate due to physical or psychological trauma.

4. If removed from the US, the applicant will suffer extreme hardship involving unusual and severe harm.

5. The applicant must be admissible to the US or eligible for a waiver of specific grounds of inadmissibility. In the case of the latter, Form I-192 (waiver application) must be submitted along with the application for the T visa.

Required Forms and Documents

To apply for T nonimmigrant status, the applicant must complete and submit Form I-914 and also include a personal statement describing the trafficking the applicant is or was subjected to.

In addition, using Form I-914 Supplement B, the applicant must attach evidence that they have complied with any reasonable request for assistance from law enforcement as required by Section 107 of the Act or, if not, evidence demonstrating that they qualify for an exception or exemption under the same provision. Other forms of evidence, including records of communication with law enforcement agencies, court documents, police reports, and news articles, may also cover this requirement.

Finally, the applicant must include evidence to demonstrate that they are either admissible to the US or eligible for a waiver of inadmissibility. In the case of the latter, Form I-192 must be submitted for the waiver request.

Fees

No fee is required for filing Form I-914 or Form I-914A. However, any other forms, such as Form I-765, Application for Employment Authorization, or Form I-192, Application for Advance Permission to Enter as a Nonimmigrant, that are filed along with the main application will require payment of the corresponding fee unless a fee waiver is requested.

Family Members of T Nonimmigrant Status Holders

In the event that the applicant's family members—namely, the applicant's parents, children, or unmarried siblings under eighteen (18) or the children of any age or marital status of the applicant's qualifying immediate family members—are in present danger of retaliation because the applicant escaped from trafficking or because the applicant cooperated with law enforcement, these individuals may also be granted T nonimmigrant status.

In the event that the applicant's family members are not in present danger of retaliation, only the applicant's spouse, unmarried children under age twenty-one (21), parents, and unmarried siblings under age eighteen (18) may be granted T visas. If the applicant is twenty-one (21) or older, only their spouse and unmarried children under twenty-one (21) may apply. To file for a qualifying family member, Form I-914 Supplement A, Application for Family Member of T-1 Recipient, must be submitted.

Benefits of a T Visa

Under Section 107 of the VTVPA, T visa holders are eligible for benefits and services under any US federal or state program or activity to the same extent as foreign nationals admitted to the US as refugees under Section 207 of the Immigration and Nationality Act (INA). These benefits include cash assistance, food stamps, and job training.

Apart from these benefits, T visa holders are eligible for an Employment Authorization Document (EAD) so that they can work in the US during their stay. The principal T applicant will be granted an EAD upon approval of the I-914 and will not need to submit a Form I-765, Application for Employment Authorization, unless the individual is also applying for deferred action. To request employment authorization for qualifying family members, Form I-765 may be submitted either together with Form I-914 Supplement A or at any time afterward.

It should also be mentioned that applicants who qualify for the T visa category may also qualify for the U visa category; however, a T visa is not as stringent. For example, a T visa does not require a law enforcement certification to be provided as evidence while a U visa does. Also, unlike T visa holders, U visa holders are not eligible for federal benefits.

Adjustment of Status to Permanent Resident

T visa holders may also apply for US permanent residence (green card) by submitting Form I-485, Application to Register Permanent Residence or Adjust Status. Note that, to qualify, the applicant must:

- Have been physically present in the US for a continuous period of at least three (3) years in T nonimmigrant status, or a continuous period during the investigation or prosecution, whichever is less.
- Be a person of good moral character.
- Have complied with any reasonable request for assistance in the investigation or prosecution of trafficking during their stay under T status or, if not, demonstrate that they would suffer extreme hardship involving unusual and severe harm if removed from the US.
- Be admissible to the US or, if not, be eligible for a waiver under Section 212 of the INA.
- For more details on the adjustment of status process (Form I-485), see Chapter 7.

3. Special Immigrant Visa for Afghan Nationals (SIVA)

Overview

The US Congress established the SIVA program as a part of the Afghan Allies Protection Act of 2009. This program is intended to protect Afghans who have worked for the US government in Afghanistan and are at risk because of their service.

In July 2021, the Emergency Security Supplemental Appropriations Act extended this program and reduced the required length of qualifying employment service from two (2) years to one (1) year. The Act of 2021 also allows certain Afghan nationals who are surviving spouses and children of US government employees abroad to obtain "special immigrant" status.

The following is an overview of the steps required to obtain a Special Immigrant Visa for Afghans (SIVA).

- Step 1 - Collect Chief of Mission (COM) Documents
- Step 2 - Scan Collected Documents
- Step 3 - Submit Documents
- Step 4 - Receive Decision
- Step 5 - Submit Petition
- Step 6 - Initiate NVC Processing
- Step 7 - Complete Online Visa Application (DS-260)
- Step 8 - Collect Documents
- Step 9 - Scan Collected Documents
- Step 10 - Submit Documents
- Step 11 - Attend Visa Interview

- Step 12 - Arrive in the US

Eligibility

Afghan nationals are eligible for the SIVA program if they:

- Were previously employed directly by the US government in Afghanistan or with a company that had a contract or subcontract with the US government in Afghanistan;
- Worked for the qualifying employer for at least one (1) year between October 7, 2001, and December 31, 2023; and
- Face threats to their safety because of their employment with the US government.
- OR
- Are the surviving spouse or child of a former US government employee who had applied for Chief of Mission (COM) approval (see Afghan Allies Protection Act § 601(1)(C)).

Application Process and Documentary Requirements

The steps to apply for a Special Immigrant Visa for Afghans (SIVA) are as follows:

1. Apply for Chief of Mission (COM) approval by sending an email to AfghanSIVApplication@state.gov and attaching scans of the following documents:

- A completed Form DS-157, Supplemental Nonimmigrant Visa Application. This form is available online at travel.state.gov/content/visas/English/forms.html.

- The applicant must complete the entire form and include start and end dates for all employment as well as any academic or military history.
- A copy of passport or *taskera* (with English translation)
- Biographic data and a copy of the employee badge (if available)
- Letter from the Afghan employer's human resources (HR) department
- Letter of recommendation or evaluation from the direct, senior supervisor or person currently occupying that position in Afghanistan, or a more senior person if the direct supervisor has left the employer or the country
- Statement explaining threat(s) received due to employment with the US government in Afghanistan

2. Complete Form DS-260 visa application.
3. Attend consular interview and complete security checks.
4. Receive visa stamp in passport and travel to the US.

Note: Many SIVA applicants have been evacuated from Afghanistan to other countries and will need to apply for their visas at a US consulate or embassy in a third country.

Timeline

The timeline for SIVA processing can vary, and it is subject to change based on various factors, including the volume of applications and the complexity of individual cases. While specific timelines cannot be guaranteed, efforts are being made to expedite the processing of SIVA applications due to the urgent circumstances many applicants face.

Supporting Documents

The following are the general supporting documents typically required of all SIVA applicants:

- Proof of Employment: Documentation demonstrating the applicant's employment or affiliation with the US government or military in Afghanistan. This may include employment verification letters, contracts, or other official documents.
- Identification Document: Valid passport, national identification card, or other official documents that establish the applicant's identity.
- Biographical Information: Details such as full name, date of birth, and contact information for the applicant and their immediate family members.
- Relationship Documents: Documents that establish the relationship between the applicant and their immediate family members, such as marriage certificate, birth certificate, or adoption papers.
- Military Records (if applicable): Military service records or related documentation for applicants who have served in the Afghan military or security forces.
- Medical Examination Results: Medical examinations conducted by an approved panel physician to assess the applicant's health and vaccination status.
- Security and Background Checks: Security and background checks on the applicants are done as part of the SIVA application process. While the specific

details of these checks are not publicly disclosed, they are necessary to ensure the safety and security of the US.

In addition to these general supporting documents required of all applicants, there are several specific required documents that only the principal applicants will need to submit in support of their SIVA application. These documents may include:

- Recommendation Letters: Letters from supervisors, colleagues, or other individuals who can attest to the applicant's employment, skills, and contributions while working with or on behalf of the US government in Afghanistan. The letters should highlight the applicant's professionalism, reliability, and dedication.
- Proof of Language Proficiency: Depending on the specific role and position held by the applicant, evidence of language proficiency, particularly English language skills, may be required. This could include language test results, certificates, or other documentation.
- Employment Contracts or Work Orders: Copies of employment contracts, work orders, or official agreements that outline the terms and conditions of the applicant's employment with the US government or military in Afghanistan. These documents help establish the nature and duration of the employment relationship.
- Proof of Work Duties and Responsibilities: Any documentation, such as job descriptions, performance

evaluations, or work records, that provides detailed information about the applicant's specific duties, responsibilities, and contributions supporting the US mission in Afghanistan.

- Proof of Threat or Persecution: Supporting evidence demonstrating the applicant's risk of facing threats, persecution, or retaliation due to their association with the US government or military. This can include threatening letters, reports of incidents, or other relevant documentation.

Bars to Eligibility

Certain bars to eligibility for SIVA may prevent an individual from qualifying for the program. Some of the standard bars include:

- **Security Concerns:** If an applicant poses a security risk or has been involved in activities that raise concerns for US national security, they may be barred from receiving SIVA.
- **Criminal History:** Applicants with certain criminal convictions or involvement in serious crimes may be ineligible for SIVA. The severity and nature of the offense can impact the eligibility determination.
- **Fraud or Misrepresentation:** Applicants who provide false information or engage in fraudulent activities during the application process can be barred from SIVA. It is essential to provide truthful and accurate information throughout the application process.
- **Health-Related Grounds:** Applicants with certain contagious diseases or conditions that threaten public

health may be barred from receiving SIVA. A medical examination is conducted as part of the application process to assess the applicant's health status.

Application Denial

If a Special Immigrant Visa for Afghans (SIVA) application is denied, the applicant will be notified of the denial and provided with the reasons for the decision. The steps or options available following a denial depend on the circumstances and grounds for the denial.

There are two main options after a denial:

1. **Reconsideration or Appeal:** In some cases, applicants may have the option to request reconsideration or to appeal the denial. This typically involves submitting additional evidence or addressing deficiencies in the original application. The process for reconsideration or appeal varies depending on the agency responsible for processing the SIVA application.

2. **Reapplication:** If the denial is not subject to reconsideration or appeal, or if the applicant's circumstances have changed, they may have the option to submit a new SIVA application. However, it is essential to carefully review the reasons for the denial and address any issues or concerns before reapplying.

Benefits

SIVA recipients are eligible for the same resettlement assistance and other benefits as refugees admitted under

USRAP and the Department of State's Reception and Placement (RandP) Program. To participate in the RandP Program, the applicant should submit a Refugee Benefits Election Form and an SIV Biodata Form (DS-0234) along with Form DS-260.

Other benefits for SIVA holders:

- Resettlement in the US: SIVA provides a pathway for eligible Afghans to seek refuge and resettlement in the US, ensuring their safety and protection.
- Lawful Permanent Residency (Green Card): Successful SIVA applicants are granted US lawful permanent residency, commonly known as a "green card." This allows them to live and work in the country permanently.
- Potential Path to US Citizenship: After five (5) years of residing in the US in lawful permanent resident status, SIVA recipients, like most lawful permanent residents, are eligible to apply for naturalization (US citizenship) if they meet certain requirements (see Chapter 7 for more details on applying for naturalization).

Additional Points Regarding SIVA

Expedited Processing: Recognizing the urgent circumstances faced by many SIVA applicants, measures have been put in place to expedite the processing of SIVA applications. These measures help to streamline the immigration process and ensure that eligible individuals can relocate to the US as quickly as possible.

Dependents: SIVA allows eligible applicants to include their immediate family members (spouse and unmarried children under twenty-one (21) years of age) as dependents on their visa applications. If the primary applicant is found to be eligible, their dependents can accompany them to the US.

Access to Resettlement Assistance: Once in the US, SIVA recipients and their eligible dependents may have access to various resettlement assistance programs. These programs aim to support their integration into US society by providing services such as language classes, job placement assistance, and access to healthcare.

Supportive Organizations: Numerous organizations and advocacy groups have been collaborating with the US government to facilitate the SIVA process. These organizations provide resources, guidance, and assistance to SIVA applicants, helping them navigate the application process and address any challenges they may encounter.

Humanitarian Commitment: The SIVA program reflects the USA's commitment to fulfilling its humanitarian obligations and ensuring the safety and well-being of Afghan nationals who have worked alongside forces or government entities of the US. It acknowledges the valuable contributions of these individuals and provides them with an opportunity for a secure and prosperous future.

4. Asylum Process for Afghan Nationals in the US

Overview

The Operation Allies Welcome (OAW) initiative allows Afghans paroled into the US to apply for asylum if they have been persecuted or fear persecution in their home country based on:

- Nationality
- Race
- Religion
- Membership in a particular social group
- Political opinion

Immigration Parole: What is it and who can get it?

To be eligible under the "Allies Welcome" program, Afghan nationals must have been paroled into the US. Parole is technically not an immigration status but rather a temporary state for foreign nationals seeking to enter the US without the promise of long-term residence. It is a form of entry that allows certain individuals to stay in the US temporarily, often for humanitarian reasons.

Parole can be granted in numerous ways, including at land ports of entry (like those along the southern US border) or through a specific parole program. The Immigration and Nationality Act states that parole may be granted on a "case-by-case basis for urgent humanitarian reasons or significant public benefit." Many Afghans have been granted humanitarian parole since the summer of 2021. To remain in the country lawfully, parolees must either apply for asylum, pursue another immigration pathway, or try to extend their parole before it expires.

When to Apply for Asylum

Qualified individuals must apply for asylum within one (1) year of their most recent entry to the US unless they can show changed circumstances that materially affect their eligibility for asylum or extraordinary circumstances directly related to the delay in filing their asylum application.

For example, a parolee under Operation Allies Welcome may be eligible for the "extraordinary circumstances" exception to the one-year filing deadline if they file for asylum while their parole is still valid. If they file their asylum application after their parole expires, they may still qualify for an exception to the one-year filing deadline if they filed for asylum within a reasonable period after the expiration of their parole.

Other Immigration Options for Afghans

In addition to asylum, Afghan parolees may pursue other immigration pathways such as a Special Immigrant Visa for Afghans (SIVA), Temporary Protected Status (TPS), adjustment of status based on an immigrant petition, or any other benefit or protection for which they may be eligible.

How to Apply for Asylum

To apply for asylum, the applicant must first complete Form I-589, Application for Asylum and Withholding of Removal, and follow the instructions carefully. Form I-589 can be found online at: https://www.uscis.gov/i-589.

Categories of Eligibility for Afghan Asylum in the US

Category 1:

1. A citizen or national of Afghanistan, or a person without nationality who last habitually resided in Afghanistan, who
2. Was paroled into the US between July 30, 2021, and Sept. 30, 2022, and
3. Whose parole has not been terminated.

Category 2:

1. A citizen or national of Afghanistan, or a person without nationality who last habitually resided in Afghanistan, who
2. Was paroled into the US after Sept. 30, 2022, and

- Is the spouse or child of an individual who meets Category 1 above, or
- Is the parent or legal guardian of an individual who meets Category 1 above and is determined to be an unaccompanied child as defined under 6 USAC. 279(g)(2), and

3. Whose parole has not been terminated.

Afghan parolees are entitled to expedited processing of their asylum applications, however, to ensure USCIS is aware that it is an expedited case, the following additional steps should be taken:

1. If the applicant is submitting a Form I-589, they should address the envelope according to guidance in the "Where to File" or "Special Instructions" section (whichever applies) on the webpage for Form I-589, Application for Asylum and Withholding of Removal.

2. Mark "Attn: OAW" anywhere on the front of the envelope.

3. On page one (1) of Form I-589, Part A.I., Question 19c, they should write their current status followed by "(Parole)" in the "status" field. For example, if the applicant entered the US with an "OAR" status, they should write "OAR (Parole)" in the "status" field.

4. Include their most recent date of entry in the "date" field on page 1 of Form I-589, Part A.I., Question 19c.

If Form I-589 is properly completed, and the authority determines that the applicant meets the eligibility criteria for Category 1 or 2 above, they will forward the application for expeditious processing under Section 2502(c) of the Act.

Application Fee

There is no fee for Form I-589.

Required Supporting Documents

The applicant must provide the same type of documents as other I-589 applicants (see Chapter 5 section on "Filing for Asylum").

Family Members

The applicant may include their spouse and unmarried children under age twenty-one (21) as dependents on the asylum application, as long as the family members are in the

US when the application is filed or before the application is decided. Any eligible family members must be present with the primary applicant at the asylum interview.

Employment Authorization Document (EAD)

Applicants may apply for an EAD as an Afghan parolee if they were paroled into the US for urgent humanitarian reasons or reasons of significant public benefit under the Immigration and Nationality Act (INA) 212(d)(5) on or after July 30, 2021.

Applying for an EAD

Eligible applicants must file Form I-765, Application for Employment Authorization, online or by mail. Applicants who are Afghan nationals paroled into the US due to the humanitarian crisis in Afghanistan do not have to pay the filing fee for the initial or replacement EAD.

Legal Representation at Asylum Interview

Applicants may bring their own attorney or accredited representative to the asylum interview at no cost to the US government.

Interpreter at Asylum Interview

If an applicant cannot proceed with the asylum interview in English, USCIS may require them to use a USCIS-contracted interpreter. If a USCIS-contracted interpreter is unavailable, USCIS may, at their discretion, allow the applicant to bring their own interpreter for the asylum interview.

Applications for Asylum After One Year

All asylum applicants (including Afghans) must file within one (1) year of entering the US. However, Afghan parolees may qualify for an exception to the one-year filing deadline if they can meet certain criteria.

Applications for Asylum After Parole Has Expired

If an Afghan parolee submits an asylum applicant after their parole time has expired, USCIS will still accept the application and schedule the applicant for an interview. At the interview, in addition to discussing the reason for applying for asylum, the asylum officer will ask why the applicant did not file the application sooner. Based on the responses, the asylum officer will determine if the applicant meets the criteria of a changed or extraordinary circumstance and if the delay in applying for asylum is reasonable, given the circumstances.

Criteria for Approval of Afghan Asylum

The asylum officer will evaluate the information provided in the application filing materials as well as during the asylum interview together with other information that may be available. The officer will use this information to determine:

1. If the applicant meets the definition of a refugee.
2. If the applicant is barred from a grant of asylum.
3. If the applicant merits a grant of asylum as a matter of discretion.

Bars to Obtaining Asylum: Polygamous Marriages

Polygamy is the religious practice or historical custom of having more than one (1) spouse at the same time. Polygamous marriages are legal under Afghan law, but they are illegal in all states of the US. Individuals should not continue to practice polygamy once in the US.

Generally, USCIS will only consider the first marriage of a polygamous marriage valid for immigration purposes. If an applicant continues a polygamous marriage they were in before coming to the US or begins a new polygamous marriage in the US, USCIS may deny their immigration application or petition.

Denial of Asylum Application

If, after the interview, an applicant is found to be ineligible for asylum but still holds valid status or parole in the US, USCIS will send the applicant a Notice of Intent to Deny (NOID). This notice will explain the reason or reasons the applicant was found ineligible for asylum. The applicant will then have the opportunity to dispute these reasons and provide additional evidence to support their asylum application. (See Chapter 7 for additional information about responding to a NOID.)

If an applicant is found to be ineligible for asylum, and they do not hold a valid immigration status or parole or they are not qualified to remain in the US at the time of the asylum office's decision, they will be placed in removal proceedings. USCIS will refer the asylum application to an immigration judge (IJ), who will reevaluate the merits of the asylum application. (See Chapter 5, Defensive Asylum Applications.)

Processing Time

USCIS is expediting the processing of asylum applications filed by certain Afghan applicants. For these applications, USCIS will conduct the initial asylum interview within forty-five (45) days of filing. If there are no exceptional circumstances, USCIS will complete the final adjudication within one hundred and fifty (150) days of filing.

USCIS Immigrant Fee

USCIS generally requires a fee to process the associated immigrant visa packets and produce the physical "green cards." Through Sept. 30, 2025, USCIS will not charge an immigrant fee to Afghan nationals, however, after this date, it will be necessary to refer to the USCIS website for the most current information.

To learn more about the Operation Allies Welcome (OAW) program and its provisions for Afghan nationals, visit: www.uscis.gov/allieswelcome

5. VAWA Self-Petition

Overview

The Violence Against Women Act (VAWA) was passed by Congress in 1994 to create a special route to lawful immigration status for victims of domestic abuse who are reliant on their abusers to file immigrant petitions for them. VAWA enables those who have suffered abuse at the hands of a US citizen or lawful permanent resident immediate family member to apply independently for immigration status, protecting the victims from potential exploitation in the family-based immigration process.

Under normal circumstances, the foreign spouse, child, or parent of a US citizen (USC) or the foreign spouse or child of a lawful permanent resident (LPR), must have a petition filed on their behalf with USCIS by their USC or LPR relative ("petitioner") to obtain permanent residence. The petitioner retains control of the process until the foreign national ("beneficiary") obtains lawful permanent residency. VAWA changed this procedure to allow foreign national victims of abuse to obtain permanent residence status through a qualifying family relationship without the participation or control of the abuser. Hence, the VAWA self-petition was created.

What to Prove

VAWA self-petitioning is very similar to filing a normal family immigration petition (see Chapter 4) but with some additional requirements. The self-petitioner must prove the validity of their relationship to the abuser. They also must prove they are of "good moral character" and have suffered "battery or extreme cruelty" at the hands of their USC or LPR relative—as defined by Congress in the immigration law.

Eligibility Requirements (Spouses)

To be eligible for self-petition as the spouse of a US citizen or lawful permanent resident, the foreign national must comply with at least one (1) of the following requirements.

- Be currently married to a US citizen or lawful permanent resident who is abusive.
- Be divorced from a US citizen or lawful permanent resident spouse within the past two (2) years.
- Have married a US citizen or lawful permanent resident believing their partner was unmarried but found out later that they were married.
- Have married a US citizen who then died within the past two (2) years.
- Have married a US citizen or lawful permanent resident who lost or renounced their immigration status within the past two (2) years due to domestic violence.

Evidence of "Good Faith" Marriage

In addition to meeting one of the above criteria, the foreign national spouse must prove that the marriage creating the qualifying relationship was made in good faith.

There is no one (1) particular type of evidence required to prove that the marriage was made in good faith, however, some common pieces of evidence include the following:

1. A written statement from the foreign national explaining how the relationship developed and why they decided to marry their spouse.
2. Birth certificates of any children together.
3. Photographs of the couple at different times and in different locations.
4. Evidence of the couple's courtship, such as text messages, call records, emails, and physical cards/letters.

5. Evidence of shared financial assets or responsibilities, such as joint tax returns, joint property ownership, joint leases, joint bank accounts, joint credit cards, and shared insurance plans.
6. Statements from friends or family with knowledge of the relationship or reasons for marrying.

Notes on Children/Stepchildren

1. To qualify to self-petition as the abused child of a US citizen or legal permanent resident, the self-petitioning child must be unmarried at the time of filing the self-petition and remain unmarried until it has been approved.
2. The stepchild of an abuser may also self-petition, but they must be unmarried and under twenty-one (21) years of age.

Application Process

There are two (2) steps to applying for lawful permanent residence (green card) through a VAWA Self-Petition.

First, the foreign national self-petitioner must file Form I-360 together with supporting evidence with USCIS. Second, the self-petitioner will need to submit Form I-485 (Application for Lawful Permanent Residence) together with certain required documents.

In the event that the self-petitioner is classified as an "immediate relative" (spouse, parent, or unmarried child under twenty-one (21) years of age) of a US citizen, they can combine these two steps into one and file the I-360 and the I-485 together or "concurrently." If the self-petitioner does not fall into the classification of "immediate relative" of a US citizen (for example, the spouse of an LPR) they must file Form I-360 first, and then, if approved, wait for their priority date to become current before submitting the I-485 application.

What to Include with Form I-360

1. A written declaration describing the relationship, the abuse the petitioner suffered, the petitioner's good moral character, and anything else relevant to proving eligibility.
2. Other evidence of the abuse, such as police or hospital records or court-issued protective orders.
3. For petitioners fourteen (14) years of age and older, police clearance records showing the petitioner's criminal record (or lack thereof) and any other evidence that the petitioner is a person of "good moral character." Note: Police certificates should be obtained from the police department of any town where the petitioner has lived for more than six (6) months during the three (3) years prior to petitioning.
4. Proof that the abuser is a US citizen or lawful permanent resident.
5. Proof of the qualifying relationship to the abuser (marriage and/or birth certificates).
6. Proof that the petitioner resided with the abuser.
7. A cover letter describing how the petitioner meets each requirement and outlining the evidence submitted to prove it.

All VAWA petitions must be filed with the Nebraska Service Center, regardless of the region of the US where the petitioner resides.

Note: USCIS will never interview a petitioner about their VAWA petition, nor will the petitioner be asked to testify about the abuse in court or any other setting. USCIS will decide whether to grant the self-petition solely based on the written evidence submitted. This is why it is very important to provide sufficient evidence.

Processing Time

VAWA processing times change considerably depending on the volume of petitions and other factors, so it is difficult to predict how long a self-petition that is filed at any given moment will take. The USCIS regards that around eighty (80) percent of the cases are completed within thirty-nine (39) months.

Fees

There is no fee required to file Form I-360 (paper filing). Currently, the fee to file Form I-485 is $1,450, however, this fee can be waived if the applicant can satisfy certain conditions.

6. Temporary Protected Status (TPS)

Overview

Temporary Protected Status, or TPS, is a special protection that allows foreign nationals from certain countries who are already in the US to remain in the US temporarily due to a humanitarian crisis in their home country—such as an armed conflict or a natural disaster—which would make it difficult for these individuals to return to their home country at that moment.

Eligibility Requirements of TPS

To be eligible for TPS, an applicant must:

1. Be a national or a habitually stateless resident of a TPS-designated country.
2. Have been continuously physically present in the US since their country's TPS designation.
3. Have continuously resided in the US since the date specified by the Secretary of Homeland Security; and
4. Pose no threat to the US for nefarious, criminal, or national security-related reasons, as determined by the relevant US agency.

An applicant may **NOT** be eligible for TPS if they:

1. Are found inadmissible as an immigrant under applicable grounds in INA section 212(a), including non-waivable criminal and security-related grounds.
2. Are subject to any of the mandatory bars to asylum. These include but are not limited to participating in the persecution of another individual or engaging in or inciting terrorist activity.
3. Fail to meet the requirements for physical presence needed to demonstrate continuous residence in the US.
4. Fail to meet the initial or late initial TPS registration requirements.

Forms to Be Completed for the TPS Application

1. Form I-821, Application for Temporary Protected Status
2. Form I-765, Application for Employment Authorization. Though it is not necessary to file Form I-765 at the same time as the TPS application, it may help an individual to receive the Employment Authorization Document (EAD) faster. Nonetheless, applicants may also apply for an EAD at a later time.

Required Documents in Support of an Application

1. **Proof of identity and nationality** (e.g., copy of passport, copy of birth certificate with photo identification, copy of any national identity document with a photograph and/or fingerprint issued by the country of origin, copy of baptismal certificate if it indicates nationality, copies of medical or school records if they have information supporting a nationality claim from a TPS country, copies of other immigration documents showing nationality and identity.
2. Proof of date of entry into the US (e.g., I-94 card)
3. **Proof of continuous residence in the US** (e.g., employment records, pay stubs, rent receipts, utility bills, medical records, attestations by a church, union, or other official organization that knows the applicant.
4. **Police and court records** if ever arrested, charged, or convicted of a crime.

Note: The more evidence the applicant can show to support the application, the better.

Application Procedure

1. Applicants can submit Form I-821 online via the USCIS website (uscis.gov) or by mail to the corresponding address on the TPS page of the USCIS website.
2. When applying, the applicant must include the required supporting documents (listed above).
3. Within three (3) weeks after applying, the applicant will receive a receipt notice from USCIS.
4. USCIS will then send applicants over fourteen (14) years of age an appointment notice to have their biometrics captured at a nearby Application Support Center (ASC).
5. On the date of the ASC appointment, the applicant must bring (a) a nationality and identity document accompanied by a photograph (such as a passport and national identity card), (b) the I-821 receipt notice, (c) the ASC appointment notice, and (d) the Employment Authorization Document (if any).
6. While adjudicating the TPS application, USCIS may send the applicant a Request for Evidence notice (RFE) asking for additional documents to establish their eligibility for TPS. (See Chapter 7 for more information about responding to an RFE).
7. Upon completing all the formalities, USCIS will notify the applicant whether their request for TPS is granted or denied. If USCIS approves the initial TPS application, they will send the applicant an approval

notice with an attached I-94 Arrival/Departure Record as evidence of their TPS.

Note: An applicant can also request to be notified by email or text message of the USCIS approval of Form I-821 by including a completed Form G-1145, E-Notification of Application/Petition Acceptance, with the I-821 application.

Registration Timeline/Program Duration

An applicant who enters the US after the date of TPS designation for their country generally may not apply for TPS at that time. A country's designated TPS period is usually six (6), twelve (12), or eighteen (18) months and can be extended at the discretion of the Secretary of Homeland Security.

Cost

When applying for TPS for the first time, the applicant must pay a $50 filing fee for Form I-821. There is an additional $30 fingerprinting (biometrics) fee for applicants over age fourteen (14). If they cannot afford the fee, they may apply for a fee waiver by submitting Form I-912, Application for Fee Waiver. In the case of re-registering for TPS, there is no fee for Form I-821.

Application Processing Time

The current USCIS processing time for TPS applications is approximately one hundred and eighty (180) days.

Benefits of Being Granted TPS:

- Successful applicants can legally live in the US for a specific, temporary period.
- They can apply for a work permit in the US.

- They can apply for a permit to travel abroad and return to the US.
- They will be protected from DHS detention and deportation.

NOTE: TPS does not provide a path to lawful permanent resident status, US citizenship, or any other long-term immigration status.

What Happens if TPS is Denied?

1. The applicant may appeal to the USCIS Administrative Appeals Office (AAO) with a request to reconsider their application. However, the applicant can only appeal to the AAO if it is specifically mentioned on the denial notice that they can appeal the decision within thirty (30) days. For more detailed information about administrative appeals, see Chapter 6.
2. If the applicant cannot appeal because they were placed in removal proceedings as a result of the denial, the applicant can ask the Immigration Judge to adjudicate their TPS application.
3. The applicant may also file a Motion to Reconsider with the USCIS Service Center. For this, they must submit Form I-290B, Notice of Appeal or Motion.

Probable Outcomes After Expiration of TPS

As mentioned, a country can be designated for Temporary Protected Status for a period of six (6), twelve (12), or eighteen (18) months. When this period expires, there are three (3) probable outcomes:

1. **Re-designation and Extension of TPS:** This means that nationals from the TPS-designated country who did not apply for TPS in the previous period can do so now for the first time, and nationals currently holding TPS can renew their status.
2. **Extension of TPS:** In this case, only nationals currently holding TPS can renew their status. Those who did not apply for TPS previously do <u>not</u> have the opportunity to apply at this time.
3. **Termination of TPS:** The status of all current TPS holders from that country will expire.

The Department of Homeland Security announces the future status of a country's TPS designation sixty (60) days before the end date of the current designation period.

The information provided above is intended to help readers better understand the process. However, consulting a professional immigration attorney will give interested applicants a better and clearer idea of their options.

7. Victims of Criminal Activity: U Visa

Overview

The U visa status was introduced in the year 2000 to encourage foreign nationals who were victims of crime in the US to support local law enforcement officials in the investigation and prosecution of these crimes without fear of being deported. The U visa includes victims of domestic violence, stalking, sexual assault, felony assault, and other crimes.

While the U visa is considered a nonimmigrant visa status, it does offer the option for recipients to obtain work permission upon approval and apply for lawful permanent residence (a green card) after three (3) years of continuous residence in the US in U status.

Requirements and Preconditions of U Visa

Victims of any of the following crimes could qualify for a U visa if the crime took place in the US: rape, torture, trafficking, incest, domestic violence, sexual assault, abusive sexual contact, prostitution, sexual exploitation, stalking, female genital mutilation, being held hostage, peonage, involuntary servitude, slave trade, kidnapping, abduction, unlawful criminal restraint, false imprisonment, blackmail, extortion, manslaughter, murder, felonious assault, witness tampering, obstruction of justice, perjury, or fraud in foreign labor contracting as well as the attempt, conspiracy, or solicitation to commit any of the crimes mentioned above.

However, just because a foreign national was the victim of one of these crimes does not mean that they automatically qualify for a U visa.

To be eligible for a U visa, the applicant must meet the following additional requirements as well:

1. The applicant must get a certification from law enforcement or another certifying agency that says all the following:

   a. The applicant is a victim of one of the approved list of U visa crimes;

    b. The crime took place in the US, including US territories and possessions, or on a US military base;

    c. The applicant has information about that crime; and

    d. The applicant was helpful, is being helpful, or is likely to be useful in the criminal investigation or prosecution of that crime in the future.

2. The applicant must also establish that:

    a. They suffered "substantial physical or mental harm" from the crime; and

    b. They are not barred from entering or receiving status in the US based on any of the grounds of inadmissibility. Note: The "grounds of inadmissibility" is a long list of crimes and other acts that could prevent a foreign national from getting status or entering the US. If one or more of the grounds of inadmissibility apply to the applicant, they must request a waiver to qualify for a U visa. It is up to USCIS to decide whether the applicant merits a waiver after weighing the pros and cons of the case.

Common Questions

1. What is a "certification from law enforcement" and how can one get it?

The following officials and agencies may be able to provide the law enforcement certification (Form I-918, Supplement B) that is necessary for a U visa application:

- Federal, state, or local law enforcement agencies
- Prosecutors
- Judges
- Other authorities that are responsible for the investigation or prosecution of criminal activity, such as Child Protective Services and federal and state agencies that do workplace investigations, such as Equal Employment Opportunity and the Department of Labor

If the applicant has reported the crime to a law enforcement agency, then the applicant (or their attorney) can request the certification from that law enforcement agency. An increasing number of law enforcement agencies are familiar with the U visa program and have employees who oversee reviewing certification requests. Other agencies may not be as familiar with U visas, in which case an immigration attorney can be helpful in obtaining the certification.

Furthermore, a law enforcement agency can provide the certification regardless of the status of the criminal case. For example, even if an arrest was never made in the applicant's case, the agency could still sign the certification based on the applicant's report. In a similar vein, law enforcement can sign the certification even if the accused suspect was found not guilty.

2. What does "substantial physical and mental harm" refer to?

USCIS will consider several factors when deciding whether the harm to the applicant (victim) was "substantial," including any permanent or severe harm to the victim's appearance, health, or physical or mental well-being. Substantial harm can be demonstrated through the victim's statement and supporting evidence, such as medical reports, declarations from mental health providers, and statements from professionals, friends, or family who helped the victim after the crime.

For example, the victim's therapist or physician can submit a declaration explaining the connection between the crime and the harm the victim has suffered, especially if it is difficult for the victim to articulate the details in their declaration.

U Visa Application Required Forms and Documents:

1. Form I-918, Petition for U Nonimmigrant Status
2. Form I-918 Supplement B (Law Enforcement Certification)
3. Form I-192, Application for a Waiver of Ground(s) of Inadmissibility, if needed
4. Form I-765, Application for Employment Authorization
5. Personal statement from the applicant describing how they were victimized. The personal statement is the most significant supporting document as it is the best opportunity for the applicant to make their case for a U visa
6. Evidence that the applicant suffered "substantial physical or mental harm" such as medical reports, declarations from mental health providers, and statements from professionals, friends, or family who helped the applicant after the crime occurred.

7. Any additional evidence (other than the law enforcement certification) that the applicant has been helpful to law enforcement and is willing to continue to be useful if needed. This can include evidence of information provided to law enforcement during the investigation or a willingness to testify in court in the future.

8. Any additional supporting evidence to show that the applicant is eligible for U visa status.

Fees and Processing Times

There is no fee required to file a U visa status application (Form I-918). Some related forms and processes have fees (such as the applications for employment authorization and inadmissibility waiver), but, depending on the applicant's income or financial need, those fees can be waived.

The processing time of a U visa application depends on various factors, such as the type and complexity of the case and the workload of USCIS. In addition, there is a statutory cap (limit) of 10,000 U visas that may be granted to principal applicants each year, which may increase the waiting time. Currently, it is taking anywhere from eighteen (18) months to four (4) years to process a U visa application.

Validity of U Visa

U visa status is granted for four (4) years. In rare cases, the U visa status can be extended beyond the four (4) years, but only if a) additional time in the US is necessary due to "exceptional circumstances," b) the certifying agency provides a new certification explicitly stating that the victim's presence in the US is required beyond the four (4) years, or c) the U visa holder has a pending I-485 application for adjustment of status.

However, as previously mentioned, after three (3) years in the US in U status, U visa holders are eligible to apply for permanent resident status (a green card) and, as such, may not require any extension of their U status.

Work Permit on U Visa

After approval of the U visa application, a U visa holder will receive a work permit valid for four (4) years. Due to lengthy processing times and limited visas in this category, some applicants (and their qualifying family members) may be eligible for interim employment authorization while their application is pending.

Applying for Family Members

U visa applicants may petition for U status for their close family members as "derivatives," however, the principal applicant must be approved for U status before they may petition for derivative family members. If the applicant is over twenty-one (21) years of age, they can petition for their spouse and any unmarried children under age twenty-one (21). If the applicant is under twenty-one (21) years of age, they can petition for their spouse and children as well as their parents and any unmarried siblings under age eighteen (18).

Adjustment of Status to Permanent Resident

U visa holders may apply for US permanent residence (green card) by submitting Form I-485, Application to Register

Permanent Residence or Adjust Status. Note that, to qualify, the applicant must:

- Have been physically present in the US for a continuous period of at least three (3) years in U nonimmigrant status.
- Have complied with any reasonable request for assistance from law enforcement while in U status.
- Be admissible to the US or, if not, be eligible for a waiver under Section 212 of the INA.
- For additional details on the adjustment of status process (Form I-485), see Chapter 7.

Chapter Four:

Miscellaneous Processes

———————— ⬛ ————————

This final chapter contains a compilation of common processes that foreign nationals and their US sponsors in a variety of nonimmigrant and immigrant visa categories may be required to go through (or choose to go through) at some point on their US immigration journey.

1. Admission Requirements for International Students (F-1 or J-1)

Overview

When foreign nationals want to study at the university level in the US, they must apply for either an F-1 (student) or a J-1 (exchange visitor) visa. This chapter focuses on the specifics of the F-1 visa, in particular, options for employing an F-1 student. For more information on the J-1 visa, see Chapter 2.

First, to obtain an F-1 visa, a US university that is approved by the Student Exchange Visitor Program (SEVP) must issue a document known as Form I-20 (or simply, an I-20), which outlines the study program details and duration. Most US universities require admission into a study program before issuing an I-20. Additionally, universities need proof of financial support from the students to show their ability to cover tuition, living, and health insurance costs in the US. The I-20, which includes a SEVIS number, is necessary for applying for the F-1 visa at a US embassy. The visa application is usually completed online and followed up by an in-person interview. When an interview waiver is available, document submission may be done through Dropbox.

If students plan to bring their spouse and/or minor children, these family members must obtain an F-2 visa. Students are required to show they have sufficient funds to cover their family members' living and medical expenses in the US as well. Because the visa process can take some time and may experience delays, students should initiate the process at least one (1) year before their program begins.

After obtaining the F-1 visa, students can enter the US up to thirty (30) days before their program starts. They must show their visa and I-20 at the port of entry. Upon arrival, they will receive an electronic I-94 which shows their F-1 status and allows them to stay in the US for the duration of their educational program. The program's duration can be modified through updates to the I-20—a process handled by the school. Each school has one or more Designated School Officials (DSOs) who monitor and assist with registration, employment, and other procedures that students must follow to maintain their status. The DSO can also make changes to the SEVIS record, for example, extending or shortening program end dates based on academic progress.

General Admission Requirements for International Students

Each academic institution in the US has its own admission standards. However, they all have some requirements in common. Both international undergraduate and graduate students must have the following criteria to be admitted to US colleges and universities:

- High school diploma
- Bachelor's degree or its foreign equivalent (if applying for a graduate program)
- English proficiency test score (TOEFL, IELTS, Duolingo Test, or any other approved test)
- Transcripts of previous academic records
- Statement of purpose
- Letter of recommendation
- Proof of financial solvency
- Curriculum Vitae (CV) or resume
- SAT or ACT score (for undergraduate students)
- GRE/GMAT score (for graduate students)
- Valid passport
- Writing sample

2. Rules and Regulations for International Students (F-1 Visa)

Overview

International students studying in the US must comply with various regulations to maintain their visa status and ensure successful academic progression.

Here are some of the key regulations and requirements for international students in the US:

Maintaining Full-Time Enrollment: F-1 visa holders are generally required to maintain full-time enrollment during the academic year, which typically means taking a minimum number of credit hours, as defined by the institution.

Work Authorization: Students can work on-campus for a limited number of hours per week during the academic year and full-time during school breaks if they receive proper authorization from their DSO. Optional Practical Training (OPT) and Curricular Practical Training (CPT) are other forms of work authorization available to F-1 students, each with its own rules and regulations.

Reporting Changes: Students are required to report any changes in their personal information, such as a change of address, to their DSO within ten (10) days. Failure to report changes in personal information can result in immigration issues.

Visa Renewal: Students must ensure that their F-1 status is valid at all times. They can usually do this by ensuring that they have a valid I-20. If the I-20 is about to expire while they are in the US, they can apply to extend or change their status before their grace period expires without the need to leave the US or apply for a new visa. Also, the expiration of the visa stamp itself has no impact on a student's status as long as their I-20 is valid. However, if the student does leave the country, they may need to renew their visa at a US embassy or consulate in order to re-enter.

Program Completion: Students are generally allowed a sixty (60) day grace period after the completion of their program to either depart the US, apply for OPT, change their status to another status, or transfer to another institution for a new program. Staying beyond this grace period without proper authorization violates visa status.

Health Insurance: Many universities require international students to have health insurance, so it is essential to maintain valid health coverage throughout the academic year.

Academic Progress: International students must maintain satisfactory academic progress. Falling below the minimum grade point average (GPA) or failing to make adequate progress toward degree completion can result in academic probation or termination of visa status.

Travel and Reentry: Students should be aware of travel and reentry requirements. When traveling outside the US, they should always carry the required documents, including a valid passport, visa, and I-20. They should also check the visa requirements for the country they plan to visit.

Social Security Number (SSN): International students can apply for an SSN if they have employment authorization such as OPT or CPT, but it is not a requirement for all students to have an SSN. Students should always check with their educational institution on this matter.

Taxes: Understanding US tax laws and filing requirements is important, especially if students receive income from any source in the US.

DOS and USCIS Regulations: The Department of State (DOS) and the United States Citizenship and Immigration Services (USCIS) govern various aspects of international student regulations. Staying informed about their guidance is crucial.

International students should work closely with their DSO to ensure compliance with these regulations and promptly address any questions or concerns regarding their immigration status and responsibilities. Violating these regulations can have serious immigration consequences, including the potential loss of status and ability to remain in the US.

3. Naturalization Application (Form N-400)

Overview

An application for naturalization (N-400) is the process by which US lawful permanent residents, also known as green card holders, can apply for US citizenship through naturalization. Becoming a US citizen offers numerous benefits, including the right to vote, access to specific job opportunities, and the ability to petition for certain family members to immigrate to the US.

Basics of the N-400 Application Process

The N-400 application process involves several stages, including completing the application form, gathering supporting documents, attending a biometrics appointment, and appearing for an interview with US Citizenship and Immigration Services (USCIS).

Below are the key steps involved:

1. **Form N-400:** The applicant must accurately and thoroughly complete Form N-400, Application for Naturalization. This form can be obtained from the USCIS website (www.uscis.gov) or by visiting a local USCIS office.

2. **Filing the Application:** The applicant must submit the completed Form N-400, together with the required supporting documents (see below) and filing fee, to the appropriate USCIS service center.

3. **Biometrics Appointment:** The applicant will be scheduled for a biometrics appointment at a local USCIS Application Support Center (ASC) after the N-400 application is received. At this appointment, fingerprints and facial scans will be taken to run background checks.

4. **Interview:** Once the biometrics process is complete, the applicant will be scheduled for an interview with a USCIS officer. The officer will assess the applicant's eligibility for naturalization, including language proficiency and knowledge of US government and history.

5. **Oath of Allegiance:** If approved, the applicant will be scheduled to attend an Oath of Allegiance ceremony, officially becoming a US citizen.

Eligibility Requirements

To ensure a smooth N-400 application process, the applicant must adhere to the following requirements:

- Be at least eighteen (18) years old at the time of applying.
- Have been a lawful permanent resident (green card holder) for at least five (5) years (or three (3) years in the case of an applicant who obtained their permanent residence through a US citizen spouse) before filing the N-400 application.
- Have had continuous residence in the US for the required period of five (5) years (or three (3) years for the spouse of a USC).
- Have maintained a physical presence in the US for at least half of the required continuous residence period (preferably, with no single departure greater than six (6) months).
- Demonstrate good moral character, including disclosing all criminal history, demonstrating compliance with US tax laws, and providing other relevant information.
- Be able to read, write, and speak basic English.
- Have a basic understanding of the US government and history (civics knowledge).

Required Documents

- Copy of the applicant's permanent residence card (green card) both front and back.
- Two (2) passport-sized photographs meeting USCIS specifications.
- Certified copies of relevant court documents if the applicant has been arrested or convicted.
- Evidence of complying with continuous residence and physical presence in the US requirements.

- Proof of marital status (if applicable).
- Any previous marriage termination documents (divorce or death certificates) for the applicant and/or spouse.
- Filing fee payment in the form of a check, money order, or cashier's check made payable to US Department of Homeland Security or by credit card or debit card using Form G-1450, Authorization for Credit Card Transactions. Note: filing fees and acceptable forms of payment may vary depending on whether the application is filed by mail or online.

Conclusion

The N-400 application process enables qualified lawful permanent residents to obtain US citizenship through naturalization. By meeting all the requirements and providing the necessary documents, applicants can successfully make this final step along the path to becoming citizens of the US.

4. Diversity Immigrant Visa Program (DV Lottery)

Overview

The Diversity Immigrant Visa Program, also known as the "DV Lottery" or the "Green Card Lottery," is an initiative by the United States government to promote diversity within the US immigrant population. As stipulated by Section 203(c) of the Immigration Act of 1990, this program aims to provide an opportunity for people from countries with historically low rates of immigration to the United States to obtain US permanent residency. Up to 55,000 diversity visas are awarded each year through a random selection process, allowing winners and their dependent family members to live and work permanently in the United States.

Employers may wish to notify prospective employees (and their spouses) from eligible countries about the DV Lottery program, as it is free to register and may provide a faster and less expensive alternative to US permanent residence (a green card) than through an employment-based petition or other means.

Advantages and Disadvantages of the DV Lottery

The Diversity Visa (DV) Lottery provides a unique opportunity for individuals from eligible countries to obtain a green card. Lottery winners and their families can have access to better education, more job opportunities, and a higher quality of life in the US. The program is free to enter, making it accessible to people from various economic backgrounds, and the application process is relatively straightforward.

However, the DV Lottery program also has a few disadvantages. The chances of being selected are quite low due to the extremely high volume of applicants every year, which can be disappointing. For those who are selected, the immigrant visa process can be stressful and time-consuming, as it involves submitting extensive documentation, undergoing medical examinations, and appearing for interviews. Additionally, applicants must be cautious of scams and fraudulent agencies that promise guaranteed selection in exchange for large sums of money. However, being aware of these issues can help interested applicants to plan accordingly.

Eligibility Criteria

To participate in the DV lottery, applicants must meet two (2) primary eligibility criteria:

1. **Country of Origin**: Applicants must be natives of countries with historically low rates of immigration to the United States. Each year, the US Department of State publishes a list of eligible countries. The aim is to diversify the immigrant population in the US by giving opportunities to people from underrepresented nations.

2. **Note:** An applicant who is not from one of the eligible countries may still be eligible to apply if (a) their spouse is from one of the eligible countries and/or (2) one or both of their parents were born in or were legal residents of one of the eligible countries at the time the applicant was born. See below for a complete list of eligible and non-eligible countries for the DV-2026 Program.

3. **Education or Work Experience**: Applicants must have either a high school education or its equivalent or two (2) years of work experience within the past five (5) years. Additionally, the work experience should be in an occupation that requires at least two (2) years of training or experience. This requirement ensures that the applicants have the necessary skills and/or education to integrate successfully into the US

workforce and support themselves and their families in the US.

Every year an official guideline on the Diversity Immigrant Visa Program is published. Reading the entire instruction manual is suggested for better understanding.

The instruction manual for the DV-2026 Program can be found at the following link: https://dvprogram.state.gov/

Eligible Countries/Areas for the DV-2026 Lottery

- **Africa:** Algeria, Angola, Benin, Botswana, Burkina Faso, Burundi, Cameroon, Cabo Verde, Central African Republic, Chad, Comoros, Congo, Cote D'Ivoire (Ivory Coast), The Democratic Republic of the Congo, Djibouti, Egypt, Equatorial Guinea, Eritrea, Eswatini, Ethiopia, Gabon, Gambia, Ghana, Guinea, Guinea-Bissau, Kenya, Lesotho, Liberia, Libya, Madagascar, Malawi, Mali, Mauritania, Mauritius, Morocco, Mozambique, Namibia, Niger, Rwanda, Sao Tome and Principe, Senegal, Seychelles, Sierra Leone, Somalia, South Africa, South Sudan, Sudan, Tanzania, Togo, Tunisia, Uganda, Zambia, and Zimbabwe.

- Asia: Afghanistan, Bahrain, Bhutan, Brunei, Burma (Myanmar), Cambodia, Indonesia, Iran, Iraq, Israel, Japan, Jordan, Kuwait, Laos, Lebanon, Malaysia, Maldives, Mongolia, Nepal, North Korea, Oman, Qatar, Saudi Arabia, Singapore, Sri Lanka, Syria, Taiwan, Thailand, Timor-Leste, United Arab Emirates, and Yemen.

- Europe: Albania, Andorra, Armenia, Austria, Azerbaijan, Belarus, Belgium, Bosnia and

Herzegovina, Bulgaria, Croatia, Cyprus, Czech Republic (Czechia), Denmark (including components and overseas dependent areas), Estonia, Finland, France (including components and overseas dependent areas), Georgia, Germany, Greece, Hungary, Iceland, Ireland, Italy, Kazakhstan, Kosovo, Kyrgyzstan, Latvia, Liechtenstein, Lithuania, Luxembourg, Macau SAR (eligibility is through Portugal), North Macedonia, Malta, Moldova, Monaco, Montenegro, Netherlands (including components and overseas dependent areas), Northern Ireland (treated separately from the UK for purposes of the DV-Lottery), Norway (including components and overseas dependent areas), Poland, Portugal (including components and overseas dependent areas), Romania, Russia, San Marino, Serbia, Slovakia, Slovenia, Spain, Sweden, Switzerland, Tajikistan, Turkey (Türkiye), Turkmenistan, Ukraine, United Kingdom (including dependent areas), Uzbekistan, and Vatican City.

- **North America:** The Bahamas.
- **Oceania:** Australia (including components and overseas dependent areas), Federated States of Micronesia, Fiji, Kiribati, Marshall Islands, Nauru, New Zealand (including components and overseas dependent areas), Palau, Papua New Guinea, Samoa, Solomon Islands, Tonga, Tuvalu, and Vanuatu.
- **South America, Central America, and The Caribbean:** Antigua and Barbuda, Argentina, Barbados, Belize, Bolivia, Chile, Costa Rica, Dominica, Ecuador, Grenada, Guatemala, Guyana, Nicaragua,

Panama, Paraguay, Peru, Saint Kitts and Nevis, Saint Lucia, Saint Vincent and the Grenadines, Suriname, Trinidad and Tobago, and Uruguay.

Non-eligible Countries/Areas for the DV-2026 Lottery

- **Africa:** Nigeria.
- **Asia:** Bangladesh, India, Pakistan, People's Republic of China (including mainland and Hong Kong), Philippines, South Korea (Republic of Korea), and Vietnam.
- **Europe:** N/A
- **North America:** Canada and Mexico.
- **Oceania:** N/A
- **South America, Central America, and The Caribbean:** Brazil, Colombia, Cuba, Dominican Republic, El Salvador, Haiti, Honduras, Jamaica, and Venezuela.

Application Process Steps

1. **Check Eligibility:** Applicants should ensure they meet the eligibility requirements for the current DV lottery. The eligible countries can change every year depending on the volume of immigrants from each country. Applicants should also consult the official guidelines and be aware of updated rules and trends of the Diversity Visa Program.
2. **Submit an Online Entry:** Applicants should complete the DV Lottery entry form on the official DV Lottery website (https://dvprogram.state.gov/) during the registration period (usually during the month of

October). This form will require personal information, including the applicant's name, date of birth, country of birth, and details about education and/or work experience.

3. **Photo Submission**: A recent digital photograph that meets the specified requirements will also need to be provided. The photo must be in color, have been taken within the past six (6) months, and meet the specifications outlined by the US Department of State, including size, background color, and facial position.

4. **Confirmation Number**: After submitting the application and photo, the applicant will receive a confirmation number. This number should be kept in a safe place, as it will be needed in various steps of the process.

Common Mistakes to Avoid During the Application Process

Submitting Multiple Entries: Only one (1) entry per person is allowed. Submitting multiple entries will result in disqualification. Therefore, only a single, error-free entry should be submitted.

Incorrect Information: The applicant should ensure that all information provided is accurate and matches the applicant's official documents. Any discrepancies may lead to disqualification.

Improper Photo: Photos that do not meet the specified requirements will result in application disqualification.

Missing the Deadline: The applicant should be aware of the deadline and plan accordingly. It is also encouraged to submit the application prior to the final week of the entry period as heavy demand in the final week can lead to website delays. Late submissions or delays in providing additional documentation will lead to denial.

Selection Process

Each year the US Department of State selects up to 55,000 winners from a pool of millions of eligible entries. The selection process is random and conducted by a computer-based system. The diversity visas are distributed among six (6) geographic regions, with no single country receiving more than seven (7) percent of the available visas in any given year. This ensures a fair distribution of visas and promotes diversity.

Selected applicants are notified through the Entrant Status Check on the DV Lottery website. Applicants must use their confirmation number to check their status. The US Department of State does not send emails or letters to notify winners. It is the responsibility of the applicant to check the status of their entry. If selected, further instructions on the next steps will be provided on the DV Lottery website.

Post-Selection Steps

If selected, the applicant must take the following steps to apply for an immigrant visa:

1. **Form DS-260**: Each winner and any accompanying family members (spouse and unmarried children under age twenty-one (21)) will have to fill out the

online immigrant visa application form. This form collects additional information needed for visa processing, including details about their background, family, and employment history.

2. **Supporting Documents**: Along with the DS-260 form, each applicant will be required to provide specified supporting documents, such as birth certificates, marriage certificates, police clearance certificates, and passports. The list of required documents can vary based on individual factors.

3. **Fees:** Each applicant will have to pay the visa application fees. These fees cover the cost of processing the visa application and conducting the necessary background checks. While there are no fees to apply for the Diversity Visa Lottery initially, winners who wish to pursue an immigrant visa must pay a visa application fee. Fees can change every year, so consulting the latest instruction manual is advised.

4. **Medical Examination:** Applicants must also undergo a medical examination by an approved physician. The examination includes a review of their medical history, a physical exam, and any necessary vaccinations.

5. **Consular Interview:** Following the medical exam, applicants must appear for an interview at a US embassy or consulate in their home country. The interview is a crucial step where applicants must demonstrate their eligibility and intention to immigrate to the US. During the interview, applicants may be asked about their background, reasons for

applying for the DV Lottery, and plans for living in the United States. If the visa is approved, a visa stamp will be placed in each applicant's passport, which the applicant must present upon their entry to the US. The physical "green card" will be mailed to the US address provided one (1) to two (2) months after their entry to the US.

Note: Lottery winners already residing in the US in lawful status may be eligible to adjust their status to permanent resident without leaving the US by submitting Form I-485, Application for Adjustment of Status.

About the Author

Raju Mahajan was born and raised in Bangladesh. From childhood, Raju was involved with many co-curricular activities like creative writing, debate, public speaking, poetry recitation, and theatre. After obtaining his undergrad degree, he worked as an FM radio producer from 2008 to 2011.

Raju published his first fiction book in 2010 at the Ekushey Book Fair, the largest and most prestigious book fair in Bangladesh. Since then, he has continued to write and publish fiction, non-fiction, and self-help materials in both the English and Bengali languages. The main theme of his fiction books is usually social critique. His non-fiction books, on the other hand, are highly influenced by tradition, folklore, and history.

Raju is an immigration attorney by profession and is admitted to the Supreme Court of the United States. He is also actively involved in multiple for-profit and non-profit initiatives. He ran for public office and narrowly lost.

In his personal life, Raju thinks that his superpower is persistence. He is a very extroverted people person, and his favorite vacation place is in the mountains. Raju is father to a toddler daughter, and his world moves around her. For those who would like to contact him, his email address is raju@rajulaw.com.

More by Raju Mahajan, Esq.

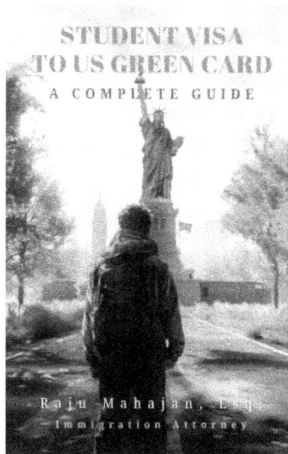

STUDENT VISA
TO US GREEN CARD
A COMPLETE GUIDE

Raju Mahajan, Esq.
Immigration Attorney

This book provides a clear path for international students in the United States, answering questions like "What steps do I take as a student?" "What immigration choices are available to me?" "Should I go with a temporary option?" "How can I obtain a permanent green card?" and many more.

Whether you are already a student in America or you are planning to make the journey to the Land of Opportunity, this book is your big-picture guide to navigating the complexities of immigration law. Learn how to prepare information for the necessary forms from an expert immigration attorney so you experience a stress-free education in the USA.

Scan the QR code below to purchase the book.